THE HAWTHORNS ENCYCLOPEDIA

ACKNOWLEDGMENTS

Thanks to John Homer (who also read the proofs) and Tony Matthews for their loan of several photographs in this book and to Kevin Grice, Dave Hewitt and Barry Marsh for the use of their original photographs, also to the many former and current players of West Bromwich Albion whom I have interviewed in the past four years.

THE HAWTHORNS ENCYCLOPEDIA

An A-Z of West Bromwich Albion FC

Glenn Willmore

MAINSTREAM
PUBLISHING

EDINBURGH AND LONDON

First published in Great Britain in 1996 by
MAINSTREAM PUBLISHING COMPANY (EDINBURGH) LTD
7 Albany Street
Edinburgh EH1 3UG

ISBN 1 85158 875 2

A catalogue record for this book is available from the British Library

Typeset in Janson
Printed and bound in Great Britain by The Cromwell Press, Melksham

A

ABANDONED. Albion have had 14 senior first team games abandoned in their history; the last domestic game to be abandoned was the FA Cup third round replay at Nottingham Forest in January 1973, called to a halt 11 minutes from time, because of heavy fog. The scores were level at 1-1, and the replay of the replay, as it were, ended 0-0. Three years before, Albion's Anglo-Italian Tournament game in Vicenza, was called off 15 minutes early after trouble on and off the pitch, with the score at 1-1. The last League game to be abandoned was the home game with the Villa in the 1965-66 season, which was called off, due to heavy rain, six minutes into the second half, with no score. The earliest a game has been called off is less than 15 minutes, which was the fate of the Albion-Bury First Division game at Stoney Lane in December 1895, when the referee found that the heavy snowfall was even worse than he had originally thought! Most controversial was the abandonment of the crucial relegation match at The Hawthorns in February 1936, when Albion were beating local rivals Aston Villa 1-0. The heavy snow saw an end to the game after just 26 minutes, and hundreds of irate Albion fans staged a demonstration outside the club offices in the blizzard, demanding their money back, and calling for the poor referee. It took considerable numbers of police to persuade the crowd to disperse. Villa won the replayed game 3-0, but still went down to Division

Two for the first time in their history.

AFRICA. Albion, as FA Cup holders, went on a six-match tour of East Africa in May/June 1968, playing in Kenya, Uganda and Tanzania. The tour was not without incident; in what has been called the 'Battle of Kampala', when Albion captain Graham Williams was sent off, there was a near riot amongst the players and spectators. A terrible tackle in the same game on winger Clive Clark effectively ended his Albion career.

23 May	Dar es Salaam Select	1-1
25 May	Tanzania (Dar es Salaam)	1-1
29 May	Uganda (Kampala)	1-0
1 June	Kenya (Nairobi)	2-1
5 June	East African XI (Kampala)	2-2
8 June	Kenya (Nairobi)	4-3

In January 1985, Johnny Giles took his side out to Tunis, in North Africa, where they drew 1-1 with the Tunisian National XI, with, coincidentally, Giles' son, Michael, scoring the Albion goal.

AGGREGATE SCORE. Albion's best win on aggregate score, i.e. over a two-legged match, is just 6-2. This has been achieved twice; against Turkish side Galatasaray, in the UEFA Cup in September 1978 – Albion won both legs by the same 3-1 score-line, and in 1966-67, they beat West Ham United 4-0 at home and drew 2-2 away at the semi-final stage of the Football League Cup. For one season, the FA Cup was played on a two-leg basis, in 1945-46, when Albion beat Cardiff City 5-1 on aggregate. They also beat Peterborough United 6-3 on aggregate in the League Cup semi-finals of 1965-66. Albion's worst aggregate defeat came against Nottingham Forest, in the second round of the League Cup in October 1982, when they lost 7-4, winning the second (home) leg after going down 6-1 at the City Ground. The most goals scored in an Albion game played over two legs is 12. In 1989, Albion lost 3-1 at home to Bradford City in the first round of the League Cup, only to pull off one of the greatest comebacks in their history, to win 5-3 at Valley Parade. With the aggregate scores tied at 6-6, 30 minutes of extra time had to be played before Albion won on the away goals rule.

Ronnie Allen

ALLEN, RONNIE. Ronnie Allen was born in Fenton, in the Potteries, in 1929, and his first club was his local side, Port Vale. He was signed by the Albion for £20,050 in 1950, at a time when the club were struggling to re-establish themselves back in the top flight after a ten-year break. He got off to a great start, scoring the equaliser at The Hawthorns in a 1-1 draw with local rivals Wolves – in front of 60,945 spectators, with another 10,000 locked outside and still tells the story of how the gatemen repeatedly refused the new signing admittance into the ground, until the club secretary was called to vouch for him! The following season, with the slightly built Allen having been tried out in four out of the five forward positions, Albion director (and former player) Tommy

Glidden suggested the revolutionary step of playing the 21-year-old at centre-forward. Allen was stunned, but was willing to try out his new role as a deep-lying centre. 'I tried to start dropping off the centre-backs, playing one-twos and getting some speed down the wing. It went very well and we got better and better and when Jesse Carver came – and went again, very quickly – it progressed from there.' New manager Vic Buckingham built a splendid team around Allen's skill and vision, which went on to win the FA Cup in 1954, and finished as runners-up in the League, and, along with Wolves, were *the* team to watch in the late '50s. Ronnie became the first serving Albion player ever to publish his autobiography when he wrote the excellent *It's Goals That Count* in 1955. A superb craftsman, passer and volleyer of the ball (and an ace penalty-taker, with either foot!) Allen won only five caps for England, but went on to play 458 times for the Albion (234 goals) before leaving for Crystal Palace in May 1961. His record of 208 League goals for the Albion stood until beaten by Tony Brown in 1979, but one record Ronnie will never lose is the unique one of being the only player to score in each of the first 20 post-war seasons, 1945-6 to 1964-5. After a successful managerial career with Wolves, Athletico Bilbao, Sporting Lisbon and Walsall, Allen returned to The Hawthorns, first as 'scouting adviser' (when he was credited with discovering Cyrille Regis), then as manager, leaving within six months after being 'lured away' to Saudi Arabia. Amazingly, he was again offered the manager's job when Ron Atkinson left for Manchester United in similar circumstances, but after one perilous season, when Albion escaped relegation in the final home game, he was 'moved upstairs' as general manager for the 1982-3 season. Once more, he returned to West Bromwich in 1991, invited back as coach by then manager Bobby Gould, and has served in an unpaid capacity under the following three managers, right up to the present day. In May 1994, he turned out in the Albion's first team for a Testimonial game at Cheltenham – at the age of 65! He has been awarded a testimonial match of his own, to be organised some time during the 1996-97 season, with a second volume of his autobiography to follow.

AMATEURS. In the League's early days, there were several amateurs who made their name amongst the ranks of the professional footballer. Two of Albion's most famous amateurs were Harold

Bache and William Jordan. Bache was a Cambridge Blue in several sports, including soccer, and played for the famous amateur side, Corinthians, as well as being capped seven times for the England amateur international side. Tragically, he was killed by a sniper's bullet whilst serving in the First World War. Jordan, like Bache, a centre-forward, played for Albion for five years at the start of the century whilst training for holy orders, later becoming a vicar in the village of Belbroughton. His frequent unavailability meant that he only played 35 games for the club – scoring 18 goals. The only amateur to play for the Albion since the Second World War was Bobby Hope, who made his Albion debut as a sixteen-year-old in 1960.

ANGLO-ITALIAN. Albion were in at the beginning of the Anglo-Italian Cup in 1970, playing at home and away to Lanerossi Vicenza and AS Roma, but failing to qualify for the final, despite being unbeaten in the four games. However, they were awarded no points for the game in Vicenza, which was abandoned because of violence on and off the field (*see* X-RATED), and it was with some surprise that they competed in the following year's competition. Against much stronger opposition (1970 Italian champions Cagliari, and reigning champions, Internazionale), Albion drew one and lost three of the four games, and failed to enter the competition again (it folded in 1976). However, the tournament was resurrected in 1992, as a replacement for the Zenith DS Cup, as a competition between English sides in the (new) First Division and Serie B Italian sides. In 1992-93, Albion qualified from their domestic group above Leicester and Peterborough, but lost all four games against Italian outfits Fiorentina, Cosenza, Padova and Pescara. Albion declined to enter the following season, but in 1995-96, with the competition reduced to eight invited clubs from each country, they tried again, and qualified, as second in their group to Ipswich Town, for the domestic semi-final, after matches against Salernitana, Foggia, Reggiana and Brescia. A 2-2 draw at St Andrews against Birmingham City in the semi-final (eventually won 4-1 on penalties) earned a two-legged domestic final against Port Vale. After a goalless draw at The Hawthorns, Vale sneaked through to a Wembley final against Genoa with two goals in the last six minutes of the second leg at Vale Park.

ANGLO-SCOTTISH. This competition originated as the Texaco Trophy (also known as the British Isles Cup, as it included some sides from Ireland) in 1970-71, when Albion lost, home and away, to Scottish First Division side, Greenock Morton. The following season, Albion beat Sheffield United over two legs, but lost to Newcastle United 4-3 on aggregate. By 1974, the competition's qualifying rounds were played as pre-season warm-up games, and although Albion needed only a draw at Peterborough's London Road in the final game, they failed to qualify from a group which included Norwich, Peterborough and Birmingham City. With the competition having lost the Texaco sponsorship by 1975, Albion once again failed to qualify for the new Anglo-Scottish Cup, from a group comprising Mansfield, Hull and Leicester City. A good win at Hull was followed by a 1-1 draw to eventual group winners Mansfield, with a 2-1 defeat at Leicester (when the new player-manager scored his first goal in Albion colours) eliminating the Albion. Middlesbrough's 1-0 aggregate win over Fulham kept the trophy in the north-east. Albion's last tilt at the the trophy came in 1976-77, when, once more, they failed to get past the qualifying stage, losing away to Bristol City, Nottingham Forest and beating Notts County at home. Forest went on to beat Orient 5-1 in the final. Surprisingly, the Anglo-Scottish tournament limped on for a number of years, as the bigger clubs gradually dropped out, with Bristol City, Burnley and Chesterfield joining the only Scottish winners, St Mirren, before the competition folded in 1981 (*see* TEXACO CUP).

APPEARANCES. Tony Brown holds the Albion record for Football League appearances; between his debut (he scored in a 2-1 win at Ipswich) on 28 September 1963 and his final game at Nottingham Forest on 12 January 1980, he made 574 appearances in the League. Including Cup games, friendlies and testimonials, Tony donned the Albion stripes in a total of 819 games, in which he scored in 312 games. His 146 Cup appearances is also an Albion club record; another one, that, in these days of easier movement of players, is unlikely ever to be beaten. Other players who have established lengthy appearance records at the club include: Alistair Robertson (total 628, League and Cups), Len Millard (625), John Wile (619), Jesse Pennington (496), Tommy Glidden (479), Joe Smith (471), Ronnie Allen (458) and Joe Carter (451).

The record for the greatest number of consecutive appearances in the Albion first team is held by goalkeeper Tony Godden, who played in 228 games in succession between August 1977 and October 1981.

ARDILES, OSSIE. As a player, Ardiles had a marvellous career. Whilst with Hurucan of Buenos Aires, he won a World Cup winners medal with Argentina before being signed, for £325,000, for Keith Burkinshaw's Tottenham Hotspur, along with team-mate Ricky Villa. The tigerish, but thinking midfielder was a revelation with Tottenham, who won the UEFA Cup and the FA Cup twice, although Ardiles missed the second Wembley triumph, having been farmed out on loan to Paris St Germain because of public hostility over the Falklands War. After seeing out his playing days at Blackburn Rovers and Queens Park Rangers, Ardiles went into management with Swindon Town, taking them to the First Division, only to see them relegated after an illegal payments scandal. He was sacked after a terrible season at Newcastle, in February 1992, when he took the Geordie side to the brink of the

Ossie Ardiles (right) and Keith Burkinshaw

Third Division, and three months later, he was approached by the Albion. The board struck lucky with the combination of Argentinian World Cup star Ossie Ardiles and dour, defensive-minded Yorkshireman, Keith Burkinshaw. As was demonstrated later, at Tottenham and Albion, either man on his own would fail, for different reasons, but the two in harness formed the perfect balance, and Albion won immediate promotion from the depths of the Third Division, albeit via fourth position, and the play-offs. Albion were a revelation in that 1992-93 season, playing fluid attacking football which delighted the crowds and set a new club League record of 85 points, with 114 goals scored by the side in League and Cups. Within weeks of Albion's 3-0 play-off final win at Wembley, Ardiles was already being lined up by Alan Sugar as the new Tottenham manager, and an acrimonious parting of the ways came in June 1993, with Keith Burkinshaw immediately appointed as his successor. Ardiles' reign at White Hart Lane was also to be brief, as his attacking principles, without the necessary defensive awareness that the experienced Burkinshaw provided, saw the Spurs defence leak goals at home and away. He was dismissed from Tottenham and, shortly afterwards, from his next position as coach at Mexican giants, Guadalajara. He is now a manager in the J-League of Japan.

ASHMAN, ALAN. After a moderate playing career with Nottingham Forest, Sheffield United and Carlisle (where he developed a reputation as a good goal-scorer in the lower divisions), Alan Ashman was given the job of managing the struggling Cumbrian side, and he gave up his job as a chicken farmer and took them from the depths of the Fourth Division, almost to promotion to the First, before being tempted away by the Albion job in the summer of 1967. Ironically, he was replacing as manager at The Hawthorns the player he formerly idolised in his time at Sheffield United, Jimmy Hagan. Widely lauded as one of the first 'track-suit managers', Ashman's relaxed, 'first name' style went down well with the vastly experienced players present at The Hawthorns at the time, especially after the authoritarian rule of Hagan. After a bit of a difficult start in the League, and an upset at Third Division Reading in the League Cup, he took the side to the FA Cup final in his first season, where they beat Everton 1-0 after extra time, in May 1968. Such was their League position as

Alan Ashman

well, at the end of the season, that if they had not qualified for the European Cup Winners Cup, they would have qualified for the Fairs Cup, by virtue of finishing eighth. Twelve months later, Ashman took the side to another FA Cup semi-final and a European Cup Winners Cup quarter-final, then, in 1970, led his side out at Wembley a second time, when they lost 2-1 to Manchester City in the League Cup final. However, as Albion became renowned as a cup-fighting side, their ageing side were slipping lower and lower in the League, and at the 1970 post-Wembley banquet, the Albion Chairman Jim Gaunt spoke of the club's need to win the League Championship. It was this ambition which caused the amiable Ashman to lose his job in June 1971, a development which he only learned about from a Greek waiter during his summer holiday. After a spell as manager in Greece, with Olympikios, Ashman returned to England to complete his job of taking Carlisle to the First Division for the first time (although only for a single season, and he resigned midway through that), finishing his managerial career at Walsall, although he later revived his career with assistant managerships at Derby County and Hereford United. Alan is now chief scout at Telford United.

ASSISTANT MANAGER. The role of assistant manager is a relatively new one at The Hawthorns. The first holder of the post was Freddy Cox, who came initially as a player-coach from Arsenal in July 1953, but graduated to become assistant manager to Vic Buckingham and, indeed, took over the reins when the manager was incapacitated after a car accident in 1954. Shortly after, Gordon Clark took over the role, which then lapsed, until Colin Addison officially occupied the post as assistant to manager Ron Atkinson from 1978 until he took over as manager in his own right at Derby County at the start of the 1979-80 season. The two men again took over the reins at the Albion from 1987 to 1988. Addison's replacement as Atkinson's assistant was Mick Brown, who resigned his post as manager at Third Division Oxford to go to The Hawthorns as understudy, and he later accompanied Atkinson to Manchester United in 1981. After that, the position lapsed, until being taken by Stuart Pearson for a while, after the arrival of new man Bobby Gould, then, when Ossie Ardiles took over from Gould, Keith Burkinshaw was installed as his assistant. When Ardiles left in 1993, Burkinshaw was promoted, with Dennis Mortimer as his assistant, and when Alan Buckley arrived in October 1994, he brought Arthur Mann with him from Grimsby to continue as his assistant.

ASTLE, JEFF. Albion's best-known player in the '60s was undoubtedly Jeff Astle – the undisputed 'King' of The Hawthorns. He was signed by Jimmy Hagan from Notts County for a giveaway £25,000. Whilst at Meadow Lane, his heading ability had been brought out by Tommy Lawton, and it was his awesome power in the air that was to be his trademark as one of the most feared strikers in the First Division. He made his debut early in the 1964-65 season, playing, not in his celebrated number nine shirt, but, instead, wearing eight, alongside John Kaye. It took a while for Jeff to settle into the team, and he played a couple of away games without getting on the mark, but in his first home game, he scored two excellent goals in a 5-1 win against local rivals, Wolves; Jeff certainly chose the ideal way to get off on the right foot with the Albion fans! Jeff scored 174 goals in 361 Albion appearances, 1964-74, topping the First Division scorers with a 25-goal haul in 1970, just before he was selected to travel with the England World Cup squad to Mexico. He was unlucky in making only five appearances for England (no goals) because he was forced to adapt to England manager Alf Ramsey's wingless style of 4-4-2, instead of the 4-2-4 more common at Albion and most other top clubs. His great year came in 1967-68, when he joined the select band of players who have managed to score in every round of the FA Cup, when he scored the only goal of the 1968 final – an extra-time winner against Everton. That winner was just one of nine goals in the Cup run – to add to the 26 he chalked up as Albion's top scorer in Division One, and he went on to breach the 20 League goal barrier in 1968-69 and 1969-70, when another great goal-scorer of the time – Tony Brown – took over as Albion's main source of goals. Intractable cartilage injuries reduced Jeff's effectiveness after 1971, when he was repeatedly hospitalised for treatment, coming back briefly to try to revitalise Albion's unsuccessful battle against relegation in 1973. He only managed six appearances in Albion's Second Division campaign of 1973-74, scoring his last Albion goal, in front of the Brummie Road that had always idolised him, against Bristol City in February 1974. He had a testimonial at The Hawthorns in the October of that year, pitting his 1968 Cup winning side (plus George Best) against the current outfit (the '68 side won!) then moved on to Dunstable Town, Weymouth, Atherstone and Hillingdon Borough, before retiring in 1977, to run his own industrial cleaning business. In the last two years, Jeff has become as famous as he was in his heyday, with his regular singing appearances on Frank Skinner's *Fantasy Football* programme on BBC2, and he released a CD of songs, from the 1970 World Cup Squad sessions, in November 1995. His book, *Striker* (Pelham, 1970), is a fascinating record of his time at the Albion.

ATKINSON, RON. After an early trial with West Bromwich Albion (instigated by chief scout Cliff Edwards) in 1954, Ron joined the groundstaff at Molineux, but soon returned to works football and an engineering apprenticeship with BSA Tools. There he was spotted by Aston Villa, but was unable to make the first team there, and was given a free transfer to Southern League

Ron Atkinson

Headington United. They soon changed their name to Oxford United where Atkinson, converted from an inside-forward to a tough, no-nonsense wing-half, who soon picked up the nickname 'The Tank'. As captain and driving force at Oxford, he helped take the club from non-League right up to Division Two during the '60s, as they replaced Accrington in the League in 1962. After over 500 appearances for Oxford, where he appeared many times in the same side as his younger brother Graham, Ron commenced his managerial career at Kettering Town in 1971, and took them to the Southern League Premier Division, attracting the interest of new League side Cambridge United in 1974. By 1977, he had taken his second Varsity side from the bottom of the Fourth Division to the brink of Division Two by the time Albion took an interest after Ronnie Allen's departure in December 1977. Albion already had a good side when Atkinson took over in January 1978, but he moulded the side in his own image, and produced an exciting, flamboyant footballing side that, but for the dreadful Big Freeze of 1978-79, would surely have won the First Division for the first time in nearly 60 years. His first home match in charge of the side was a superb 3-2 extra-time win over FA Cup holders

Manchester United, ironically, the club he was to leave the Albion for so abruptly three years later. Albion reached the FA Cup semi-final that year, only to lose out in an incident-packed match against eventual Cup winners, Ipswich, at Highbury. Before the game, Atkinson came in for a great deal of criticism from Albion supporters for allowing himself to be filmed by the BBC walking around Wembley Stadium, a factor which Ipswich boss Bobby Robson has admitted did more than he ever could to fire up his side for the game. Still, with an eventual finish of sixth place in Division One, Albion qualified for Europe for the first time in ten years, and reached the quarter-finals of the UEFA Cup the following year, going out to Red Star Belgrade on aggregate after what Atkinson himself admits as 'sheer naïvety', throwing away a home lead to go out of the competition to a very late goal at The Hawthorns. That season Albion pushed eventual Champions Liverpool all the way for the title, only to be pipped for second place minutes from the end of the season. Albion had achieved 59 points, the highest total ever managed in the First Division by a team finishing third, and qualified once again for the UEFA Cup. 1979-80 was a serious anti-climax, particularly as Atkinson had failed to hang on to key players such as Laurie Cunningham (sold to Real Madrid), Len Cantello (to Bolton) and Willie Johnston (to Vancouver Whitecaps), and at one stage, in January, Albion were looking likely candidates for relegation, until Ron blooded a new youngster, Remi Moses, into the midfield. Albion lost just two of the last 18 games and went on to finish ninth in Division One. Atkinson had spent well in an attempt to replace his departing players, bringing in Peter Barnes and Gary Owen from Manchester City, and John Deehan from neighbours Aston Villa, and those new men had begun to 'bed in' to the team by the 1980-81 season. Once again, Albion made a bid for the title, and but for an unfortunate defeat at Villa Park late in the season, might well have prevented Villa from collecting the Championship themselves. Albion finished fourth, qualifying for Europe for the third time in four seasons. However, the Albion board had not renewed Atkinson's contract, and whilst on tour with the Albion in America he was approached by Manchester United, who soon appointed him as successor to the recently dismissed Dave Sexton. Ron's departure for a 'big money' club like United would have been acrimonious enough in itself, but he chose to return to purchase the two king-pins of the Albion's midfield, Bryan Robson and Remi Moses, for a combined fee of £2.5m. Albion were never the same side after that, a fact which upset a lot of his former supporters in West Bromwich. In his five years at Old Trafford, Ron spent over £7million on new players, but despite several runners-up spots, he could not achieve the United Holy Grail of the League Championship, although they did win the FA Cup in 1983 and 1985. That would have been enough at most clubs, but Ron was sacked in November 1986, after a bad start to the League campaign. After a projected move to Athletico Madrid fell through, Atkinson, amazingly, was persuaded to return to The Hawthorns in September 1987. He managed, just, to keep the club out of the Third Division play-offs at the end of the season, although the Albion's final position of twentieth in Division Two was a new club low. Wily moves into the transfer market, notably for Arthur Albiston, Andy Gray, Brian Talbot and Chris Whyte meant that by the following season Albion had a useful squad – but Atkinson was not there long enough to appreciate it. In October 1988, when refused an extension to his remaining 18-month contract at The Hawthorns, Atkinson left for Athletico Madrid. Within 96 days, Ron was back in England, sacked by club owner Jesus Gil, despite taking the club as high as third in the Spanish First Division. Back in English football, Ron experienced his first taste of relegation, with Sheffield Wednesday, but promptly took them back to the top division – and won the League Cup, against Manchester United at Wembley. Immediately afterwards, Ron moved to Aston Villa, where he took them to runners-up in the first-ever Premier League season, then won the Coca-Cola Cup, before being surprisingly sacked by 'Deadly' Doug Ellis. He joined Coventry City as manager early in 1995.

ATTENDANCE, AVERAGE. Albion's average attendance for their entire 108-year spell in the Football League is just under 20,000 – not a bad figure considering that in their early days of membership, when they played at Stoney Lane, they never actually had a 'gate' which reached 20,000, and usually averaged around 5,000 spectators per match. Average attendances increased after the move from Stoney Lane to The Hawthorns in 1900; from 5,500 to 12,000, even though their first season at the new ground resulted in relegation. The first 20,000-plus average attendance for a season was achieved in 1913-14; two seasons later, in 1919-20 (after a four-year break during World War One) it had climbed to 30,000; the season Albion won the Football League for the only time. Attendances fell back after that, averaging around 21,000, until the post-war boom, when several best-ever seasons averages were reached – 33,379 in 1948-49, which was the year that the club regained their First Division place, increasing to 38,279, a figure which will now never be beaten. The marvellous 1953-54 season went close to this average, though, reaching 38,279. Once again, there was a gradual decline in gates as the quality of the team declined, dipping as low as 18,000 in 1962-63, but another general boom in attendances after the 1966 World Cup saw an average of nearly 28,000 in 1969-70. Relegation to Division Two meant a dramatic drop to attendance levels not seen for nearly half a century, with the 1974-75 figure down to less than 12,679; that was doubled though, by the time the First Division was reached in 1976, and there was another peak of nearly 27,000 in 1978-79, when the club finished third in Division One. Albion's declining form from then on, coupled with the general malaise in the game after the Bradford fire and Heysel, meant that Albion were losing over 1,000 spectators a season from their average gate, 1982-88, with the first season back in the Second Division bottoming out at 9,280. There was actually an increase in average attendances for the two seasons spent in the (old) Third Division, to watch a winning side, with gates in the First Division now around 15,000.

ATTENDANCE – HIGHEST. With the attendance of The Hawthorns now down to 25,800, it is hard to imagine how 64,815 spectators were squeezed into the ground for the sixth round FA Cup tie against Arsenal in March 1937. Four times has the attendance at the ground been over 60,000, and, as would be expected from a club with Albion's Cup traditions, three of those were for FA Cup ties – the highest ever League attendance at The Hawthorns (60,945) coming against the Wolves in March 1950. Away from home, not unexpectedly, six of the top seven gates have been for Albion's Wembley Cup finals (all between 90-100,000) – the exception being the UEFA Cup quarter-final match at Red Star Belgrade, which attracted 95,300 in 1979. The best attendance for an Albion away game on a Football League ground came in January 1948, when 71,853 saw the fourth round FA Cup defeat at White Hart Lane. Remarkably, Albion once attracted a crowd of 55,497 to The Hawthorns, in the '50s – for a testimonial game! It was staged to raise money for former Albion goalkeeper, Norman Heath, whose career had just been tragically cut short by a serious back injury sustained in a League game at Roker Park just after the 1954 FA Cup semi-final.

ATTENDANCE – LOWEST. The lowest gate for a League game in West Bromwich came at the club's Stoney Lane ground, on 29 November 1890, when just 405 fans saw their side lose 4-3 to Derby County. Two years later, only 607 attended the Staffordshire Derby with Stoke City and in 1896, only 506 turned up for the last game of the season against Blackburn Rovers. Attendances greatly increased after The Hawthorns ground was opened in September 1900, but even at the end of that first season in their new home, already relegated Albion could only attract 1,050 fans for the final game of a miserable campaign. In December 1993, a new record low for a senior competitive Albion game was set in Cosenza, southern Italy, when just 37 paying customers watched the Anglo-Italian Cup game. Complimentary tickets, particularly for the small number of travelling Albion fans, pushed this into three figures, but this is still a record unlikely to be beaten.

AUSTRIA. Albion went on tour to Austria in the close season of 1961, where they played out three games unbeaten against Lustenau (3-3), Linz (3-2) and Graz (2-1). Ten years earlier, for the Festival of Britain celebrations, Albion had entertained another Austrian side, SC Wacker, losing 4-3 at The Hawthorns. There was another Albion connection with Austria – the Baggies right-back in their 1892 FA Cup winning side, Magnus Nicholson. After leaving the Albion in 1894, Nicholson, a schoolteacher, went on to become national coach, and first president of the Austrian FA, becoming a pioneering force in the establishment of football in Austria. He must be the only Albion player to have a team named after him – Nicholson FC, later SC Vienna!

AUTOGLASS TROPHY. Competed for only by Third and Fourth

Division clubs (formerly the Associate Members Cup and the Freight Rover Trophy), with a lucrative Wembley final at stake, the competition was arranged in the form of a round-robin qualifying group, followed by a single-leg knockout. Albion entered for both of their seasons in the Third Division, and qualified for the knockout stage each time, losing at home to Exeter City in 1992 and away to Stoke City the following year, in front of a then record gate (outside Wembley) of 17,568.

B

BACHE, HAROLD. *See* AMATEURS.

BANKRUPTCY. Although Albion are still not in the best of health
financially speaking, their current predicament is as nothing com-
pared to the way it was at the turn of the century, when the club
came close to being wound up. The club had been relegated to
Division Two for the second time in 1904, and the 1904-05 season turned out to be the worst in the club's history, as they finished tenth in Division Two – and, for the first time, failed to
reach the FA Cup competition proper. To raise cash, the board
forced secretary/manager Fred Everiss to sell their best players,
including George Dorsett, Ike Webb and Harry Hadley, but
refused to release cash for suitable replacements. The crisis came
to a head in December 1904, when the entire Albion team agreed
to accept half wages to help the club through – it was a grand ges-
ture, but still not enough, and within months the club's bankers,
Parr's, served the club with a writ demanding full payment of their
substantial overdraft. At the time, the club was losing over £1,000
a year and a creditors' meeting on 3 March 1905 was told that
unless a 'debt holiday' could be granted for a period of two years,
then the club would have to be wound up. Fortunately, the creditors agreed to do just that, in the (mistaken) belief that the club
would regain a First Division place, and profitability, within that

time. After the meeting, the entire board resigned en bloc, signalling a return for former chairman Harry Keys and a welcome for a new director, former playing star, William Bassett. When the Birmingham *Evening Despatch* started a 'Shilling Fund' in April 1905, the worst of the crisis had passed, but the £401 raised in the West Bromwich area by rifle-shooting matches and billiard evenings was gratefully received, and the club was soon back in the black, although it took until 1911 to win promotion.

BARGAIN BUYS. Without question, Albion's best 'bargain-buy' of modern times has to be Cyrille Regis, bought from non-League Hayes for just £5,000. In 1978, the Albion turned down an offer of £750,000 from French side St Etienne for the 21-year-old. Although eventually sold for a bargain £300,000 to Coventry City in 1984, Regis, at his peak, would have commanded a seven-figure sum. In purely financial terms, Laurie Cunningham was one of the best buys – he cost £110,000 from Orient in 1977, and was sold to Real Madrid for an Albion record fee of £995,000 just two years later, which represents the best annual rate of return for any player that Albion have ever bought. In 1925, Albion paid just £2,500 to Chesterfield for Jimmy Cookson, who scored 255 goals in only 290 games for the Spireites, Albion and Swindon, including 38 goals for the Baggies in the 1927-28 season, when he scored six in one game against Blackpool. Cookson lost his place, in 1930, to a player who cost exactly half as much, from Hartlepool – and who went on to break all Albion's scoring records, including Cookson's 38 goals in a season; William 'Ginger' Richardson. An England international, 'W.G.' was a masterful goalscorer, and his thirty years at The Hawthorns (as a player and a trainer), 1929-59, were remarkable value for the paltry £1,250 fee.

BARLOW, RAY. Swindon-born Ray Barlow was spotted playing for the Wiltshire-based works side Garrards by former Albion centre-forward Jimmy Cookson, a publican in Swindon at the time. He made his Albion first team debut in wartime football, but his first League outing was an auspicious one, as he scored one of the goals in a remarkable 7-2 win at Newport County in the first post-war League season, in 1946. After some difficulty with homesickness in the following years, Ray got his big chance when he played, as an inside forward, in the last 17 games of the promotion season, in 1948-49, and indeed, he scored one of the three goals at Filbert Street which clinched Albion's promotion back to the First Division. Fairly early on in his career, Barlow was converted to a left-half, a position which he really made his own, although he did also play at centre-half and centre-forward, in emergencies. Tall, for a creative midfield player, he used his enormously long legs to pull the ball out of the air, leaving the heading of the ball almost exclusively to his fine central partner, Joe Kennedy. For nearly the whole of the '50s, Barlow ran the creative engine-room of a great Albion side, and should have won more than just one England cap, kept out of the national side, as he was, by Portsmouth's consistent, but undoubtedly less skilled skipper, Jimmy Dickinson. He was the Albion captain near the end of his time with the club, and made nearly 500 appearances for the side, and scored 50 goals, before finishing off his football career at Birmingham City, leaving West Bromwich in June 1960.

BARNES, PETER. When Laurie Cunningham was tempted away by Real Madrid in 1979, Ron Atkinson pulled off a major coup by signing, as a replacement, the man who was keeping Cunningham out of the England side – speedy winger, Peter Barnes. The deal was part of a double swoop on Manchester City which included the England Under-21 captain, midfielder Gary Owen, for a total of £1.2 million, £748,000 of which was for Barnes – an Albion record buy which still stands, more than 15 years later. Barnes, son of City's chief scout and fomer star of the '50s, Ken Barnes, had all the pace and skill of a classic winger, and ended as Albion's top scorer in his first season, 1979-80, with 15 goals. A further ten goals followed in 1980-81, most of them of the highest quality, before he was sold by new manager Ronnie Allen to Leeds United – for £930,000. Allen had no time for Barnes' apparent lack of commitment – 'He just used to graze out on the wing' – and snapped up a healthy profit for the club not long after returning for his second spell at managing the Albion. After Leeds' relegation that season, Barnes' career went into free-fall, as he moved to, amongst others, Real Betis, Coventry City, Bolton, Sunderland, Hull and both Manchester clubs. After a spell as youth development manager at Maine Road, Barnes took over as manager at Runcorn early in 1996.

William Bassett

BASSETT, WILLIAM. William Isaiah Bassett was probably the best player ever associated with West Bromwich Albion – in terms of skill and glamour, he was the George Best of his day. A fast, immensely skilful outside-right, born in West Bromwich, and attending the same Christ Church School as so many of the Albion's great pioneers, Bassett was the first Albion man to become a truly national figure, idolised by football lovers all over the country. Yet when Bassett made his first few appearances in the Albion team at the end of the 1886-87 season, he was felt to be too small and lightweight for the rigours of English football. However, the poaching of Albion's inside right, Tom Green, by Aston Villa during the summer of 1887 had left a serious vacancy in the side and Bassett took his chance well in a season that made his name, as well as that of the club, when they went on to win the FA Cup for the first time. Bassett had a great game in the Final, supplying the crosses for both goals in the win over Preston, a performance which earned him the first of his 16 caps for England (the equivalent of around 80 caps nowadays) against Ireland later that year. Remarkably, Bassett was just 19 years old when he first wore that England shirt, making him the youngest ever Albion player to achieve international recognition. Despite his wide position on the field, Bassett was also an accomplished goalscorer, recording a century of goals in around 400 appearances for the club, but his effectiveness was reduced during the early part of his career by a bizarre boycott by his striking partner George Woodhall, who, for a time, refused to pass to the young 'upstart' who was usurping his position as the club's top star! Bassett retired from playing at the peak of his career, but was unfortunate that his last game was a 7-1 thrashing by Champions Aston Villa at Villa Park in April 1899. He returned to the club during its darkest days of near bankruptcy in 1905, when he became a director, and was voted in as chairman three years later, a position he held until his death in 1937 – which ended a 51-year association with the club. His death, coming the day before Albion lost to Preston North End in the FA Cup semi-final at Highbury, was mourned by football followers all over the world. At the time, as well as being Albion chairman, Bassett was a member of the FA Council, the Football League Management Committee and the England International Selection Committee.

BATSON, BRENDAN. The first player that incoming manager Ron Atkinson bought in 1978 was the captain from his previous club, Cambridge United – former Arsenal right-back, Brendan Batson. That first buy was also Atkinson's best, as the youngster developed to become one of the best full-backs in the country, although, inexplicably, he was never capped beyond England 'B' level. He rapidly repaid his £30,000 fee many times over with so many mature performances in over 200 games for the Albion. Like his full-back partner, Derek Statham, Brendan was always available to surge upfield on an overlapping run, but rarely got into goal-scoring positions, scoring just twice for the club, most memorably a diving header against Ipswich in front of the *Match of the Day* cameras in 1981. Tragically, Batson was forced to retire from playing in 1984, after a bad injury sustained in a 6-1 defeat at Ipswich in October 1982. After several operations, he had attempted a couple of comebacks in pre-season friendlies, but his knee was clearly not up to the rigours of professional football. He was granted a testimonial by the Albion against Aston Villa, later that year, and went on to become Secretary of the Professional Footballers Association.

BAYLISS, JEM. 'Jem' (for his initials, James Edward Matthias) was an incredibly prolific centre-forward in Albion's pre-League days in the mid 1880s. Tipton-born, he signed for the Albion from local rivals Wednesbury Old Athletic in 1884, and went on to appear in all three of Albion's FA Cup finals 1886-87-88, and scored one of the two goals in the club's first FA Cup final win against Preston in 1888. Amazingly, that was one of more than a half century of goals that Bayliss scored in that 1887-88 campaign, in the fixture list of friendlies, FA Cup ties and local Cup games that was available at the time. By the time the Football League came along in 1888, Bayliss had begun to convert to right-half, and he was one of three ever-presents in the Albion's first League season, mostly in that position, but he reverted back to the for-ward line in 1889, and was the club's second highest scorer with nine goals.

Appearances were rather limited after that, and he retired in 1892, having played just 56 League games for the Albion (12 goals). The year before, uniquely, Bayliss had become a club director – whilst still a player, and he remained on the Albion board for 14 years, until the crisis year of 1905.

BELGIUM. Albion's first post-war continental tour was to Belgium and Luxembourg, in May 1946. In the first game, they lost to the Belgium National XI, 5-4, in Verviers, beat Fola Jennesse in Esc-sur-Alzette, in the Grand Duchy, by five goals to one, then drew 1-1 with top Belgian side RSC Anderlecht in Brussels. Albion's first-ever opponents in the European Cup Winners Cup were another top Belgian side, cup holders RFC Bruges. Albion lost a very physical game 3-1 in Belgium, but won another, equally unpleasant game at the Hawthorns by two goals to nil, with the Albion going through to the next round on away goals. In July/August 1974, Albion went on a two-match tour of Belgium,

Martyn Bennett

losing 1-0 at KV Mechelen, where former Albion defender John Talbut was player-manager, and winning 2-1 at another Belgian Second Division side, Diest.

BENNETT, MARTYN. Albion had two great defenders who were forced to give up the game early in the '80s – Brendan Batson and Martyn Bennett. The tall, blond Bennett was long seen as the ideal replacement for long-serving centre-half Alistair Robertson, when he signed, as an England schoolboy international, for the

Albion in 1977. He was given his First Division debut by Ron Atkinson against Everton in 1979, and gradually established himself – in a very strong side – in 1980. The Birmingham-born youngster had his best season, in terms of games played, in 1984-85, when he only missed three League games, but that was the exception rather than the rule, as injuries began to keep him out of the side more and more. And not just out of the Albion side, as he was ruled out of the England squad by injury after being called up for the first time in 1985, although he did later make the England substitutes' bench, without being called upon to play. In the four seasons, 1986-90, Martyn started just 19 games for the Albion, playing his last game in a fantastic 7-0 home win against Barnsley in November 1989. That was his 219th game in a ten-year period when, if fit, he could well have played nearer 500 games. He was granted a testimonial game against Crystal Palace the following year but, uniquely for an Albion testimonial, the game was postponed because of bad weather, and when it was rescheduled for the start of the 1992-93 season, the opponents were changed – Birmingham City obliging at The Hawthorns. Bennett was able to continue playing at non-League level, with Worcester and Cheltenham, later managing both clubs in a brief and unsuccessful managerial career.

BIRMINGHAM & DISTRICT LEAGUE. The Birmingham & District League was founded in 1889 for local sides such as Stourbridge, Brierley Hill Alliance and Smethwick Carriage Works. It began to admit the reserve sides of the big League clubs at the start of the 1892-93 season, and at one time, the second strings of Albion, Aston Villa, Wolves, Small Heath (Birmingham), along with the first teams of both Stoke and Coventry City. The competition was completely dominated by Aston Villa reserves, who won the Championship a dozen times. Albion managed the feat on just three occasions, in 1902, 1913 and 1920, and left the League the following year, joining Villa, Wolves, Birmingham and Stoke in the far more competitive Central League, comprised entirely of the reserve sides of League clubs.

BIRMINGHAM CHARITY CUP. Never one of Albion's favourite Cup competitions, the Lord Mayor of Birmingham's Charity

Cup, to give it its full title, was an invitation-only competition, staged to raise money for local charities. It was first held in 1882, with Aston Villa, who had an extraordinarily good record in the competition. Albion's first game was a 4-1 defeat at Aston Villa in April 1884, and, incredibly, it took the Albion a dozen games before they recorded their first win, an amazing 7-4 extra-time victory at home to Small Heath. Although the matches were by invitation, so that sometimes only one win was needed to reach the final, Albion did not actually achieve that until 1900, when they beat Walsall 1-0 at Aston. They then reached the final three years in succession, 1901-1902-1903 – and lost the lot, to Villa (twice) and the Wolves. In 1906 the Albion lost 4-3 to Villa in the final at Small Heath. Interest in all the local Cups was waning at this point, and from 1910 onwards, the Cup was staged as a single game, by invitation, and Albion received the call on 11 occasions in the 19 seasons up to 1932-33, winning four times (1914, 1915, 1922 and 1925) and sharing the trophy with Birmingham in 1921. Albion's last two appearances in the final of the Lord Mayor of Birmingham's Charity Cup were actually on their own ground, Aston Villa winning 3-2 and 4-0 at The Hawthorns in 1931 and 1932 respectively. In 1993 the LMBCC was revived as a tournament for local non-League sides, staged exclusively at the Moorlands Stadium in Birmingham.

BIRMINGHAM ROAD. The Birmingham Road end of The Hawthorns (or 'Brummie Road' as it is colloquially known in West Bromwich) has long been the 'popular' end of the ground, being the first part of the ground reached on foot or by public transport from the town centre. When the ground was first built in 1900, the Birmingham Road end consisted of an open bank with cinders and railway sleepers underfoot, and, incredibly, the end was not even covered until 1964, when the roof from the Handsworth stand was moved there after the current 'Rainbow' Stand was erected. At the end of the 1993-94 season, following the home League game with Grimsby Town (won 1-0), the Brummie Road fans set off on an orgy of souvenir hunting, ripping down signs and 'borrowing' the old throstle on top of the half-time scoreboard, as the Birmingham Road end was closed down prior to its demolition. Building work continued through the summer right up to Christmas 1994, and the new all-seater stand (known to the Commercial Department as the Apollo 2000 Stand, but to everybody else as the Brummie Road) was officially opened for the game against Bristol City on Boxing Day, Monday 26 December 1994, a game won 1-0 by the Albion. Matching the other new stand, at the Smethwick End, the Birmingham Road Stand was the final requirement to comply with the Taylor report for all-seater stadia – the total cost of both new stands was £4.6 million, leaving The Hawthorns with a capacity of 25,800.

BIRMINGHAM SENIOR CUP. The Birmingham County Football Association was founded in December 1875 and its County Cup, the Birmingham Senior Cup, was instigated that same season, Tipton FC being the eventual winners. Albion joined the Association at the start of the 1881-82 season, so the Birmingham Cup was actually the first competition that Albion ever competed for. Albion's first-ever Cup tie was away to Calthorpe, on 12 November 1881, a match won 3-2. Wins followed against Elwell's, Falling Heath Rovers and Notts Rangers (with Albion having to travel some way away from home turf for a supposedly Birmingham-based competition) as Albion reached the semi-final, where they lost 3-2 to rivals Wednesbury Old Athletic, at the Aston Lower Grounds. The following season, they again went out to Wednesbury OA, at the quarter-final stage, then lost in the 1884 semi-finals to Walsall Swifts, again at Aston. Revenge was gained in 1886, when the club won the competition for the first time, beating Walsall Swifts 1-0 in a final replay at Aston (after a 1-1 draw). The following year, Albion were the victims of a major upset in the competition when the holders, who had earlier, of course, reached the FA Cup final for the second successive year, lost in the final to unrated Long Eaton Rangers. The 1888 final was lost to Aston Villa, 3-2, and in Albion's fourth consecutive final, in 1889, Aston Villa were once again the victors, 2-0. Albion reached the final once more in 1892 when, having already won the FA Cup for the second time, they met Wolverhampton Wanderers at Perry Barr – and lost 5-2. Two years later, they again met the Wolves in the final, at the same venue, and drew 3-3 – with both sides declining extra-time or a replay, the trophy was shared between the two clubs. The following year, Albion gained slight revenge for their defeat by Aston Villa in the FA Cup final of 1895 by beating their close rivals 1-0

31

in the Birmingham Cup final at the Lower Grounds – in Aston! The last time that Albion's first XI competed in a Birmingham Cup Final was in February 1905 – and they suffered the club's worst-ever defeat in the final round of any competition, losing 7-2 at Small Heath. The following year, Albion went out 5-1 at home to Aston Villa in the first round, which was the last time that any of the Football League clubs routinely entered the first XI in the competition, which reverted to a Cup for local non-League clubs and reserve sides of the bigger outfits, Albion entering their reserve side in the Cup for another thirty years or so. In 1982, pressure from the Birmingham County FA meant that the 'Big Six' West Midlands clubs were forced to re-enter the Birmingham Senior Cup, but, on payment of a 'fine' were allowed to field their reserve sides once more. Albion had a fair record in the competition, winning the trophy three times in the space of four years, beating Bedworth United, Atherstone United and Nuneaton Borough in 1988, 1990 and 1991, respectively.

BISSEKER, WILLIAM. A strong, aggressive centre-forward in the club's early days, when the Strollers were still very much based around George Salters Works, Bisseker scored a good number of goals in his five-year career as a player. Although he only played in very few official competitive games, he scored regularly in the friendlies that were arranged with primarily local sides at that time (1879-84). On retiring at the very early age of 21, Bisseker became Albion's official club umpire, in the days when the referee was backed up on the field of play by a nominated official from each side, a role which he carried out for many years, until the two-umpire system was abolished.

BOOKS. A considerable number of books have been written about the club over the years. The first full history of the Albion, *Football in the Black Country*, was written by Peter Morris in 1965, whilst the second and most recent, *WBA: The First Hundred Years*, by Glenn Willmore, was published to mark the club's centenary in 1979. There was also an attempt at an annual publication, the *WBA Football Book* (1970), by Ray Matts, but the format never really took off, although it has been revived in 1995, by the publication of Sports Projects' *Albion Review*, featuring match reports and statistics from the previous season. The club's statistician,

Tony Matthews, has written two books of a statistical nature, *The Centenary A-Z of Albion* (1979) and *Albion, A Complete Record* (1987, revised 1993), whilst *WBA: 100 Great Matches* (1994), also by Glenn Willmore, covers the best 100 games in the club's history, as well as featuring interviews with many Albion players and managers. All but the last two are now out of print. There have also been several autobiographies by players and managers who have served the club, notably *It's Goals That Count* (1954) by Ronnie Allen and *Striker* (1970) by Jeff Astle. Other autobiographies of interest, and covering in some depth their time at The Hawthorns, have been written by Ron Atkinson, Willie Johnston, Bryan Robson and Bobby Robson.

BOWSER, SID. Sid Bowser was a Handsworth-born lad who signed for the Albion from non-League Willenhall Town in July 1908, after an unsuccessful trial with Birmingham. He made his debut at outside-left in spectacular fashion, scoring two goals in a 7-0 demolition of Grimsby Town in January 1908. Back in the side midway through the following season, Bowser played in just over half the League games, but still ended the season as joint top scorer with 16 goals. The following season, 1910-11, Bowser was the kingpin in the promotion side which won the Second Division Championship, as he was again top scorer with 22 goals in 38 League games. In 1911, 1912, 1913, Sid was not so successful in the rarefied heights of the First Division, scoring just 14 times in 60 games, although he did help get Albion to runners-up spot in the FA Cup in April 1912. A year later, he left the Albion over a dispute concerning wages, and played in Ulster for six months with Belfast Distillery, rejoining the Baggies in February 1914. Converted to a goal-scoring centre-half, Bowser had another great ten years at The Hawthorns, winning a First Division Championship medal in the 1919-20 side, and significantly contributed to that success with ten goals from the centre-half position, including a hat-trick in one game against Bradford City in September 1919. He won his solitary England cap, against Ireland, later that year. Bowser played nearly 400 games for the Albion, scoring 72 goals (19 as a defender) before leaving the club for a second, and final time, in August 1924, when he signed for Walsall – and Albion still picked up a useful £250 fee for him!

BRADLEY, DARREN. Darren Bradley was brought to The Hawthorns by his first manager, Ron Saunders, who recognised the youngster's talent when he signed him, ostensibly as a makeweight, in a deal that saw England international Steve Hunt move to Villa Park in March 1986. Bradley started his Albion career as a full-back, but injuries, and a falling out with new manager Ron Atkinson, limited his appearances, and it was not until 1990, under Brian Talbot, that he really established himself as a first team regular. When Albion were relegated to Division Three in 1991, Bradley found himself being used as a defensive-minded midfielder, and stood out as the kingpin in Ossie Ardiles' diamond formation during the promotion season of 1992-93, when Darren led the team as captain to a Wembley play-off victory against Port Vale. An excellent passer of the ball, a tough competitor, with a long throw-in, Bradley lacked the pace needed at the highest level, and, after a crucial knee operation in 1993, which reduced his pace still further, was released on a free transfer to Walsall at the end of the 1994-95 season, as part of Alan Buckley's first 'clear-outs' — just a few months short of a testimonial game for what would have been ten years' service with the club. Such was his injury record, though, that the player only averaged around 20 games per season during those ten years.

BRIBES. In 1913, Albion captain Jesse Pennington was offered, on behalf of his side, five pounds per man to 'throw' the result of an Albion-Everton game. The England international informed club secretary Fred Everiss, the police set a trap and the offender, Pascoe Bioletti – who had no connection with Everton football club – was arrested and sentenced to five months imprisonment. It emerged later that Bioletti, who was working for his father, the owner of a Geneva-based betting consortium, had also arranged a similar bribe for the players of Birmingham. Coincidentally, it was Everton who were again involved in a bribery scandal, when the *People* newspaper alleged that Everton players attempted to bribe the Albion side for a crucial League game at The Hawthorns in May 1963. A win for Everton would assure the club of the First Division Championship – and Albion lost 4-0, conceding a bizarre own goal and a penalty. The allegations remained insubstantiated.

BROWN, ALLY. Alistair Brown was signed by Albion manager Don Howe for around £60,000 in March 1972, to give some much-needed goal-scoring punch to a relegation-threatened Albion side. Ally scored on his debut in a 1-1 draw with Crystal Palace, following up with a goal in a 2-0 win at Coventry in his next game. Albion had signed the Scot from Leicester City, where he was top scorer in the Second Division Championship season in 1970-71, but the striker soon fell out of favour and languished in the Central League side for much of his early career at The Hawthorns – he only made 17 appearances in the club's first two Second Division campaigns, 1973-74 and 1974-75. His career was revitalised under Johnny Giles in 1975-76, when he started the new season in the team, playing alongside former World Cup hero Geoff Hurst for a while, before settling down into an unlikely striking partnership with the lumbering Joe Mayo, and ending as the Albion's top scorer in that promotion season, with ten League goals. Ally drifted in and out of the side over the next two years of First Division football, but suddenly came into his own under the management of Ron Atkinson. He only missed one League game in the great '78-'79 season, and once again was Albion's top goalscorer, with 18 League goals, and he was named, along with his namesake Tony Brown, as joint Midlands Player of the Year. Inconsistency was always Ally's problem though, and the goals dried up in 1979-80 – just six in 27 games – but he recovered to score ten in 31 full appearances the following season, helping Albion to a final placing of fourth, and back into Europe. A spell playing for Portland Timbers in the NASL, in May/August 1981, was considered a break in his Albion service, even though he returned to play for the club by September of the following season, thus denying the player an Albion testimonial for what was to be 11 years service to the club. Ally's last goal – and one of his best – was in a 2-1 defeat at Maine Road in December 1982. He left for Crystal Palace in March 1983, but he only played 11 games (2 goals) at Selhurst Park before moving to join Walsall in August of the same year. At Walsall and his next club, Port Vale, he maintained his career average of a goal every three games, helping the Potteries side to promotion from the Fourth Division in 1986, also, that season, making his solitary return to The Hawthorns in a 1-0 defeat for Vale in the 1985-86 League Cup. Ally retired at the end of that season, to become a

Tony Brown

publican in West Bromwich. He now runs the Albion's Official Supporters Club in Halfords lane, opposite The Hawthorns.

BROWN, TONY. 'Mr Albion', Tony holds the club records for most League appearances (574) and most goals (218) in a 20-year career at The Hawthorns that saw him win both the FA Cup and League Cups with the club. Originally a goal-scoring wing-half, Brown gave notice of what was to come when he scored on his debut in a 2-1 win at Ipswich Town in September 1963; it took him a couple of seasons to establish himself in the team, but he was a first choice from 1965 to 1979, topping the club's scoring chart time after time, and forming a lethal combination with centre-forward Jeff Astle, whose goalscoring mantle he gradually assumed. A versatile player, Brown played in all the midfield and forward positions at the club, as well as making the role of penalty-taker his own – a position that the club have yet to fill with any confidence, as Brown rarely missed any of the 60 or so spot-kicks he attempted. That power of shooting also won him many goals from free-kicks all around the penalty area, another area in which Albion have been lacking since his departure. His most spectacular goal was scored in a 2-1 defeat in the FA Cup at Sheffield Wednesday; a volley over his shoulder against former England goalkeeper, Ron Springett, but the goal that is most fondly remembered by Albion fans is the one he scored at Oldham – his home town – which won Albion promotion back to Division One in 1976. In 1970-71, his 28 goals made him the First Division's top scorer, and helped to win him a long overdue England cap – against Malta, it was his only international selection at full level, although he was also recognised for Young England and the Football League XI. Expected to take more defensive responsibilities after the arrival of Don Howe as manager in 1971, Brown's goals dried up to some degree, although he was still top scorer in the side for all four years of Howe's reign at the Albion. By 1977, his scoring rate had dropped to eight goals a season, but he was given a new lease of life by the arrival of the attack-minded Ron Atkinson, who described Brown as 'the best goal-scorer I have ever worked with, bar none'. During the 1977-78 season, Atkinson's first at the club, Brown was top scorer, for the last time, with 23 League and Cup goals, and he weighed in with 14 valuable strikes in Albion's great '78-'79 season. Brown played the last of his nearly 900 senior appearances for the club in 1980, moving to Torquay in October 1981 after the arrival of new Albion manager Ronnie Allen. Tony returned to The Hawthorns as a coach after the appointment of Johnny Giles as manager in 1984, but left after Giles' resignation in October 1985 to take up a post as assistant manager to his former Albion team mate, Gary Pendrey, at Birmingham City. Granted a testimonial match in 1974 (unusually, featuring a combined Albion/Villa side against a Blues/Wolves team), he was promised a second testimonial by Ron Atkinson; that promise has now been honoured by the club and will go ahead some time in 1997.

BUCK, FRED. Like Sid Bowser, Freddy Buck was another skilful inside-forward around the turn of the century who had two separate spells with the Albion, before converting to perform splendidly as a centre-half later in his career. The difference was size –

Buck stood just five feet four inches, very small, particularly in those days, for a centre-half. He signed from Stafford Rangers in November 1900, and, like Bowser, had a spectacular start, scoring in a 7-2 win over Bolton Wanderers, although he failed to score again in his other six outings that season, as Albion were relegated to the Second Division for the first time. In Albion's successful Second Division Championship season of 1901-02, Buck only played twice – the disastrous first match defeat at home to Glossop and a late-season game against Burton United, in appalling conditions, when he scored the winning goal, and after just 13 games in the First Division, he left the club. He first went to Liverpool, then, with the Merseysiders retaining his registration, to Southern League Plymouth Argyle, returning to The Hawthorns in April 1906. His second spell was far more successful, as he ended the 1906-07 season as second top scorer with 20 goals in 32 games, and was top scorer with 18 goals the following year. In 1908-09 he was second in the goalscoring stakes, and joint top in 1909-10 with Sid Bowser, and chipped in with a vital ten goals in Albion's promotion season the year after. By the time the club was back in Division One, Buck was beginning to play as a centre-half, where his immaculate displays took Albion to the FA Cup final in 1912. He was an automatic choice at centre-back almost up to the start of World War One, by which time he had made over 300 appearances for the club, scoring nearly 100 goals. He left for Swansea Town in May 1914, but his career was abruptly terminated by the war and he retired from the game in 1917.

BUCKINGHAM, VIC. Vic Buckingham was a cultured wing-half with Tottenham (1935-49, 234 appearances) during their lengthy spell in the Second Division. He took over as coach to the Oxbridge hybrid side, Pegasus, and took them to victory in the FA Amateur Cup in front of 100,000 at Wembley in 1951. A few months later, he was appointed manager of Bradford Park Avenue and after a useful 18 months in charge, was appointed as Albion manager to succeed coach Jesse Carver in February 1953. Buckingham revolutionised the Albion, turning them from a useful, if dour side, to one of the best attacking sides in Europe, winning the FA Cup in 1954, and, as runners-up, going within five points of the first League and Cup Double of the 20th century. There was another FA Cup semi-final in 1957, and, during his six year tenure, Albion sides usually did well in the First Division and the Cup. One season where the Albion struggled in this period was the year after the Cup win, during the 1954-55 season; but Buckingham was hardly in charge for much of the campaign. He and his assistant, Freddy Cox, were involved in a serious car crash following a testimonial game at Hereford early in the campaign. Buckingham suffered head injuries and a broken arm, and handed over to Cox until he recovered – and Albion struggled for the rest of the year. In the words of Albion stalwart, Bobby Robson, 'Buckingham was an articulate and romantic individual – a great benefit to my career'. Buckingham resigned in May 1959. He took over at Ajax of Amsterdam shortly afterwards, where he was responsible for discovering the young Johann Cruyff, and the club won the Dutch League in 1960, and the Cup in 1961. In May 1961, he took over as manager at Sheffield Wednesday, poaching Albion's then manager, Gordon Clark, as his assistant, but he was dismissed from Hillsborough in 1964, despite taking the club to the quarter-finals of the Fairs Cup. His last managerial appoint-ment in England was a brief spell at Fulham, where he gained a reputation for eccentricity, before leaving in January 1968 to take up senior positions at Ethnikos, in Greece, Seville and Barcelona, where he won the Spanish Cup in 1971. In his later years, living in retirement in Worthing, Buckingham developed Alzheimer's disease. He died on 26 January 1995.

BUCKLEY, ALAN. After a great career as a goalscorer at Walsall (sandwiched by a less happy spell at Birmingham City), where he scored a club record 174 League goals, Alan Buckley started early in the managerial stakes as player-manager at Fellows Park at the age of 28. He made a good job of being Walsall manager, taking the Midlands Cinderella side to the League Cup semi-finals and back into the Third Division, although there was an unfortunate period when his joint manager, Neil Martin, was given his job for nearly a year. In August 1986, Buckley was abruptly sacked by the new, incoming Walsall chairman, Terry Ramsden, and three months later was appointed as boss of Conference side Kettering Town, who he took to the brink of the Football League in his two years in charge. In June 1988, he took over at struggling Fourth Division side Grimsby Town, and raised them to the (old) Second Division, playing neat, entertaining, passing football, within a

Alan Buckley

very limited budget. It was for those very qualities that the Albion board approached Buckley in October 1994, following their dismissal of former manager Keith Burkinshaw, and, after an acrimonious split with the Blundell Park club, the new man took over for Albion's game at Barnsley on 22 October 1994. At the time, Albion were bottom of the First Division, but after a losing start at Oakwell (0-2), Buckley pulled the club around, without spending very much money, and secured their safety from relegation, two games from the end of the season. In 1995-96, the supporters were astonished when the side, with a much smaller squad following Buckley's money-saving shedding of excess players, managed to reach second place in the table before Christmas, but a record-breaking run of defeats in November and December sent the side plummeting down the table and into relegation trouble again.

BULL, STEVE. Steve Bull is probably the most famous 'one that got away' from The Hawthorns – and the situation was made all the worse for the fact that he was the one player who virtually saved long-time rivals Wolves from extinction in their darkest

Steve Bull

hour in the mid-'80s. Signed along with Andy Thompson from the Albion (after five full Albion appearances) for a pittance in November 1986, because Albion manager Ron Saunders thought he would never make it as a professional footballer, Bull went on to score (so far) around 300 goals for the Wolves, taking them from the lower reaches of the Fourth Division, and FA Cup humiliation by Chorley, to the massive club that they are once again, breaking all club records and winning England caps along the way. In his first two games against his former club, in 1989-90, Bull scored the winner on both occasions, and has been a thorn in the Baggies' side ever since. Albion have a sell-on clause built into the original Bull transfer deal where they stand to collect a third of any money made on a subsequent transfer, which looked as if it might pay off when Coventry City bid £2 million for the striker in 1995, but it now seems as if Bull will end his career at the club he did so much to save.

BURGESS, DARYL. After Stuart Naylor, the longest-serving player on Albion's books, and one of the few home-grown talents to make his mark in the side in recent years. He made his debut at

Daryl Burgess

Port Vale in August 1989 and has gone on to become a first choice selection for the team at either full-back or, his preferred position, at centre-half. A serious back problem kept him out for most of the 1992-93 season, but he returned to the team in March 1993 and forced the crucial McFarlane own goal at Swansea which helped Albion qualify for the Wembley play-off final – only to injure himself in the process, and miss the final. After surgery, his career-threatening back injury was finally sorted out and he has rarely missed a match since.

BURKINSHAW, KEITH. The dour Yorkshireman made his career at Fourth Division Workington, after making just one appearance for his first club, Liverpool. In his final season at Borough Park, Burkinshaw took his first steps in management as player-manager of the Cumbrian side, before moving to Scunthorpe to finish his playing career. After coaching with the Zambian national side, then Newcastle, he became coach, then manager at Tottenham Hotspur, but Spurs were relegated to the Second Division for the first time in over 20 years at the end of his first season in the job. The Spurs directors persevered with their man, and in return he took them to two FA Cup wins, in successive years, 1981 and 1982, and the UEFA Cup in 1984. In 1978, he sensationally signed the first two major soccer imports, Ossie Ardiles and Ricky Villa, to start a flood of foreign imports which still continues today, but resigned from the Spurs job, citing 'disillusionment with Spurs' business interests' as his reasons. Coaching spells in Bahrain and Lisbon followed, before a brief spell as manager at Gillingham, before he was taken from his job as chief scout at Swindon to become Ossie Ardiles' assistant manager at The Hawthorns. Burkinshaw's steadiness and defensive caution was the perfect foil to Ardiles' obsession with 'the beautiful game', usually preventing the Argentinian's attack-minded play from becoming too undisciplined at the back, and Albion had a hugely entertaining and successful 12 months with the two of them in control, winning promotion back to Division One, via the play-offs, in 1993. When Ardiles left for Tottenham in June of that year, however, Burkinshaw was given the manager's job on his own – and made a terrible mess of it. Lack of communication with the players and a general air of disinterest led to the club strug-gling in the higher division, with safety only being assured on the last day of the season, in a cliff-hanger at Portsmouth. A change of chairmanship led to Burkinshaw's dismissal in October 1994, when he was replaced by Alan Buckley, a move which led to an immediate improvement in results, and safety for another year.

C

CANADA. Albion have made five trips to North America, playing several of the games on each tour in Canada rather than the USA. The first trip was in May/June 1959, when the club took on a punishing schedule of nine games in the space of just 20 days, coast to coast across the continent. Eight of the games were in Canada. Albion scored a massive 59 goals in total, losing only one game to the British Columbia Select XI. Ten years later, at the end of the 1968-69 season, Albion travelled west again to play in the Palo Alto Tournament in California, but stopped off first to play two games in Canada, where they beat Vancouver All Stars and Victoria O'Keefes. At the end of the 1980-81 season, after Albion had finished fourth in the First Division, they jetted off for a three-match tour, playing two games in Canada, this time against NASL clubs, for the first time. They lost 2-1 to Johnny Giles' Vancouver Whitecaps then beat Edmonton Drillers 2-1. Albion have also played host to sides from Canada. Way back in 1888, Stoney Lane was the venue for a game between Albion and a touring Canadian XI; it was some surprise that the FA Cup holders could only beat 'The Colonials' by a single goal. In October 1960, The Hawthorns was the stage for a match between Albion and a touring Canadian FA XI, and there was another shock when the Canucks managed to spring a shock 1-0 win. Albion have had two Canadian players on their books. Glen Johnson, born in

Len Cantello

Vancouver, made four appearances at centre-forward in the early '70s, later playing for Vancouver Whitecaps and Vancouver Royals and winning nine caps for Canada. In the mid-'80s, Mancunian Carl Valentine, a naturalised Canadian, played 44 League games for the Albion, winning his first Canadian cap whilst with the Albion, later going on to represent his country in the Mexico World Cup finals in 1986.

CANTELLO, LEN. Powerful midfielder Len Cantello was another product of Albion's fine youth set-up during the '60s. Manchester-born, he signed professional for Albion in October 1968, making his debut as a substitute in the First Division at Ipswich two months later, and progressing enough to win a place in the League Cup final against Manchester City in 1970, whilst still just 18. Len really blossomed for the Albion after the arrival of Johnny Giles in 1975, and although he won eight Under-23 caps for England, he really should have gained full international honours in the late '70s. Mainly a midfielder, he actually wore all the outfield shirts for the club, having particularly good spells as a full-back, appearing in nearly 400 games for the Albion. His goal tally was a meagre 21, although there were some quality ones amongst them, notably the fearsome rocket of a shot in the 5-3 win at Old Trafford in 1978, which won Central TV's Goal of the Season Award. On the morning of his testimonial in May 1979, he announced to the press that he would be leaving the club immediately, under the new Freedom of Contract system, and moved for a fee of £350,000 to struggling Bolton Wanderers – and his career nosedived from there. After less than 100 games in the downwardly mobile Trotters side, he passed through a huge number of struggling clubs, including Stafford Rangers, Hereford, Bury, Peterborough (where he played against his former club in a pre-season friendly at London Road), and Northwich Victoria. From 1987 to 1989, he teamed up with his former Albion midfield colleague, Asa Hartford, as assistant manager at Stockport County. He now works in Manchester, but still assists Coventry City manager Ron Atkinson with scouting for the club.

CAPS, ENGLAND. Although Albion's last player to be capped for England was as far back as 1986, the club has a long tradition of supplying men for the England side. Albion's first English international was goalkeeper Bob Roberts, who was honoured with the first of his three caps back in 1886-87. Since then, 40 more Albion players have been capped for England, including such great names as Ronnie Allen (5 caps), Jeff Astle (5), Tony Brown (1), Billy Bassett (16), Laurie Cunningham (3), Derek Kevan (14), Don Howe (23), Cyrille Regis (4), Bobby Robson (20), Bryan Robson (13) and Derek Statham (3). Albion's most capped player for England was full-back Jesse Pennington, who won 25 caps between 1906 and 1920 – the equivalent of 90 or more in these days of regular international competitions. Bryan Robson, although only winning 13 caps whilst with the club, went on to win 90 caps in all, making him the most capped player who has ever played for the Albion. Albion's youngest ever international was Billy Bassett, who played for England against Ireland at the age of 19. John Reynolds, who won three England caps whilst with the Albion (1891-93) had earlier won five caps for Ireland whilst a player with Distillery in Ulster, his English birthplace allowing him, in those early days, to switch allegiance.

CAPS, IRELAND. The Republic of Ireland only started playing football as an independent nation in 1924 – before that date, there was just one Ireland side covering both north and south. Albion have had seven players capped for the Republic, the first being centre-forward Dave Walsh, who won the first of his 14 caps with the Albion in 1946. Soon after, Reg Ryan won 15 caps (1949-55). There was a brief resurgence in the number of Irish players at The Hawthorns in the mid-'70s when the manager of the Irish team, Johnny Giles, took over as player-manager at West Bromwich, so that at one time there were four Albion players in the Eire side (Giles, Ray Treacy, Paddy Mulligan and Mick Martin all played for Ireland against France and Poland in 1977 whilst with the Albion). Four is the highest number of internationals Albion have ever had in one national side. Albion's most capped Irishman is full-back Mulligan, who won 16 caps whilst at The Hawthorns; the last Irishman to be capped whilst with the Albion is midfielder Tony Grealish, who won the last of his ten caps whilst with the Albion against Denmark in 1986.

CAPS, NORTHERN IRELAND. Albion have had seven players capped for Northern Ireland. The first was Dave Walsh, who was a dual international, playing for both Northern Ireland and the Republic of Ireland from 1946 to 1950 – Reg Ryan also made one appearance for Northern Ireland, against Wales in 1950. Albion's most capped player for the province was centre-half Jack Vernon, who won 15 caps between 1946 and his return to Irish football in 1952. Full-back Jimmy Nicholl, although only with the Albion barely 15 months, managed to win 11 caps to reach a total of 73 appearances for his country, making him the most capped player to appear in an Albion side. Albion's last Northern Ireland international was the much criticised centre-forward Paul Williams, who made a brief appearance as substitute against the Faroe Islands in a 1-1 draw in 1991.

CAPS, SCOTLAND. Albion have only had five players capped for Scotland whilst on their books, not least because there was an unofficial 'boycott' of Scottish players by the club for over 30 years up until just before World War Two. As a result, Albion's first Scottish cap was won by 'Sandy' McNab as late as 1939. Since then, defender Doug Fraser (2 caps) and midfielders Bobby Hope (2) and Asa Hartford (6) have also won international recognition. Albion's most capped Scot was Willie Johnston, who won 13 caps between 1976 and in the 1978 World Cup finals in Argentina; that was the last cap awarded to an Albion player.

CAPS, WALES. 15 Albion players have been capped for Wales. The first to be selected was Seth Powell, who won the first of four caps in 1890. Other prominent Welsh internationals were centre-forward Stan Davies (11 caps), Walter Robbins (6) and Jimmy Murphy (15). Murphy went on to manage Wales during the '50s, in tandem with his job as assistant manager to Matt Busby at Manchester United. In the early '60s, Albion occasionally supplied both full-backs for Wales. Stuart Williams, at right-back, is the most capped Albion player of any nationality, winning 33 caps for Wales between 1954 and 1962. Left-back Graham Williams (no relation) won 26 caps between 1960 and 1969. Albion's most recent Welsh international was central defender and recent club captain, Paul Mardon, who was capped (as substitute) by Welsh manager Bobby Gould (another former Albion player) in October 1995, for the European Qualifying game against Germany in Cardiff.

CARTER, JOE. Joe was the classic inside-forward: small, wiry, intelligent – and a very good goalscorer. He played nearly 500 games for the Albion between 1922 and 1936, scoring over 150 goals. His strength was his close control, which enabled him to weave his way through the tightest defences, and which won him three full England caps. Born in 'rival' territory in Aston, Joe made his Albion debut in a 3-0 defeat at Bolton in 1922-23, alongside a young winger, Tommy Glidden, who was playing in only his third game. Both players were rested soon after that defeat, but when the right-wing combination was tried out again a year later, it started to 'click' – and a marvellous Albion partnership was born. From then on, it was rare to see an Albion team without the pair – indeed, the team went ten years with at least one of them in the side in every match. The combination helped to take Albion to the runners-up spot in the First Division in

1925, and although the team was relegated in 1927, the Carter-Glidden partnership was still there in 1931, taking Albion to their famous double of promotion and the FA Cup. In 1935, Carter struggled to find his form, scoring just five goals in 33 League appearances, and missing out on an FA Cup run to Wembley, Arthur Gale making a fine goal-scoring substitute. Gale, in fact, scored in every round of the Cup except the semi-final, but on Cup final day, was cruelly dropped in favour of a returning Carter, who had been doubtful with a serious knee injury. Carter played, but cost Albion the Cup when he broke down during the game, leaving Albion with ten fit men for much of the match, which Sheffield Wednesday won 4-2. He made another 19 appearances for Albion in 1935-36, but was transferred to Sheffield Wednesday in February 1936 – a move which was terminated after six days on medical grounds; the same right knee which had given way at Wembley the year before. After an operation, he finally moved on to Tranmere, where he stopped briefly before finishing his career at Fellows Park.

CARVER, JESSE. Jesse Carver is the great 'forgotten' manager of West Bromwich Albion – possibly because he never held that title officially. He made his name before the war as a robust type of centre-half, with Blackburn and Newcastle, but it was after the war that he became really fashionable, with his unusual ideas on training – including such modern ideas as actually working with the ball, rather than starving the players of the sight of a ball, to 'encourage them to want possession on matchdays', as so many clubs did! He perfected his methods, unusually for the time, on the continent, with the Dutch FA, Lazio and Juventus, where he won Serie A in 1950. When the Albion dismissed manager Jack Smith in 1952, they took on Carver as 'trainer-coach' in May 1952, but, under pressure from his wife, who wanted to return to Italy, and with an offer he described as 'too good to refuse', he left for Lazio in February 1953. He had done his job – his influence in training is attested to by all of Albion's senior players from that period, and he acted as a catalyst for the successful Albion sides of Vic Buckingham during the rest of the decade. The side he left behind finished fourth at the end of 1952-53, and went so close to lifting the double the year after. After leaving The Hawthorns, Carver had spells as manager at Lazio (twice), AS Roma, Genoa,

Internazionale, as well as another six unsuccessful months as Coventry City manager, before coaching at Tottenham and then Portugal and the USA.

CENTENARY. Albion celebrated their first 100 years with a number of events in August and September 1979, climaxing with a special challenge game at The Hawthorns against Dutch Champions Ajax, which, happily enough, Albion won 1-0. The date of the celebrations was based on the supposed date of the Albion's formation in September 1879, but since then, it appears that an Albion side, based upon the George Salter Works team, was playing at least a year before that date (*see* FORMATION).

CENTRAL LEAGUE. The Central League was formed in 1911 to provide a competition for the reserve sides of the top clubs in the north-west, plus the first teams of some of the aspiring non-League sides of the time. The founder members were: Liverpool, Everton, Manchester United, Manchester City, Bolton, Blackpool, Burnley, Bury, Oldham, Preston, Blackburn, and Glossop (reserve sides) and Lincoln, Burslem Port Vale, Crewe, Stockport and Southport Central (first teams). Albion's reserves joined the Central League in 1921, after nearly three decades of competition in the West Midlands-based Birmingham & District League, when the League reorganised to expel all of its non-League sides, to invite such clubs as Leeds United, Albion, Wolves, Villa, Stoke and Birmingham. Albion have played in the Central League (now renamed the Pontins Central League) ever since and, although having a difficult time in recent years, have one of the best records of any club in the competition (*see* RESERVES). Up to 1982, the bulk of the reserve games were played on Saturdays, but following the reorganisation of the Central League into two divisions that season (now three), almost all games are played midweek, and there is a trend, which the Albion have so far resisted, for many clubs to play their reserve games on the grounds of smaller clubs, to save wear and tear on the pitches. Thus Villa have been playing at Walsall, Leeds at Halifax and Wolves at Telford.

CENTRAL LINE. The *Central Line* was the official reserve and youth programme of West Bromwich Albion from 1987 until its abrupt termination at the end of 1995. Running at anything from four to 24 pages, and the forerunner of many similar reserve programmes at other League clubs, the *Central Line* ceased production late in 1995.

CHAIRMEN. Albion have had just 17 chairmen in the past 110 years. Harry Keys (chairman 1899-1903 and 1905-08) played an important part in saving the club when it looked like going out of business and his son, Major H. Wilson Keys took over the reins from 1947 to 1963 – the longest serving chairman in the club's history. Former players, rather than local businessmen or dignitaries, were prominent in the early days, with Jem Bayliss (1903-05), the great William Bassett (1908 to his death in 1937) and Lou Nurse (1937-47) all playing their part. Current Football Association chairman, Sir 'Bert' Millichip, was Albion chairman during some of their best days, 1974-83 (he is now club president). The current chairman is Tony Hale, who took over from his predecessor Trevor Summers in 1994.

CHARITY SHIELD. The Charity Shield started life as the Sheriff of London's Charity Shield, and was contested annually between 1898 and 1907 between the best amateur and professional sides in the country. In 1902, Albion had been invited to replace Southampton in the match that year against Tottenham, but could not arrange a date. In 1920, First Division Champions Albion were again invited to meet the Second Division Champions – Tottenham, ironically – at White Hart Lane. Albion won the game 2-0, in front of 38,168 people. Albion never again won the Championship, but from 1930, the game, taken over by the Football Association, was revived as a pre-season pipe-opener between the Champions and the FA Cup winners of the previous season, so as FA Cup winners, Albion competed for the trophy again in 1931, 1954 and 1968. In 1931, the game was still held at a neutral ground, early in the football season, and in October 1931 Albion took on the mighty Arsenal at Villa Park – and lost 1-0, although they went on to complete a fine League double over the Londoners that first season back in Division One. By 1954, the match was played on the home ground of the League Champions and, after an eight-goal thriller at Molineux, the trophy was shared for six months each between the Albion and the

Wolves. Albion's heavy defeat at Maine Road in 1968 was one of the biggest losses in the history of the competition, but was partially explained by the fact that goalkeeper John Osborne was injured, and was replaced in goal by full-back Graham Williams. That was Albion's last appearance in the Charity Shield, which has been played as a pre-season game at Wembley for the last 20 years.

CHINA. Albion were the first professional Western side to tour China, in the close season of 1978. As part of a trade delegation, they played four games behind the Bamboo Curtain, plus one in Hong Kong, winning all five, with Cyrille Regis scoring in every game. The high point of the tour was a game against the Chinese national side in Peking, which Albion won 2-0. The tour was featured on a BBC2 documentary later in the year, and in 1979, when the Chinese came to Britain, they lost 4-0 at The Hawthorns in a 'friendship friendly' match, the second half of which was broadcast live on BBC2.

CLARK, CLIVE. Probably one of the fastest wingers ever to have worn the navy blue stripes, Clive Clark was an essential part of Albion's attack-minded side during the '60s. A superb goalscorer as well as provider, Clive was a virtual ever-present in the Albion side from the time he signed from Queens Park Rangers in January 1961, to the time he returned to the same club in June 1969, his final year at The Hawthorns being cursed with serious injury problems sustained whilst on tour with the Albion in East Africa in 1968. He was a member of the side that reached Cup finals in three successive years, 1966, 1967, 1968, collecting winners medals in the League Cup final against West Ham in the first of those, and in the FA Cup final against Everton in the last. In the run to the League Cup final of 1967, Clark became the only player ever to score in every game of the tournament, including the two goals that gave Albion such a handsome lead at half time at Wembley against Queens Park Rangers, only to see the match end in disappointment when Albion lost 3-2. In around 350 games for the Albion, Clark scored nearly a hundred goals and was Albion's top League goalscorer in 1966-67, with 19 goals. His second spell at QPR was brief, but he won a Third Division Championship medal at Preston, then assisted Southport and

Telford, before winding down his career in the NASL with Washington Diplomats and Philadelphia Fury. He is now in rather poor health, having returned to live in his native Yorkshire.

CLARK, GORDON. A right-back with Southend United and Manchester City before the war, Gordon Clark started his managerial career as player-manager of Waterford, followed by moves to Distillery and Aldershot once his playing career had finished. Surprisingly, Clark resigned his post at the Recreation Ground in 1955, to become Albion's chief scout, later becoming assistant to Vic Buckingham, and taking over from him as manager in June 1959. He did well to continue Buckingham's fine work, and Albion finished fifth at the end of the 1959-60 season, but after a terrible start the following year, he quit in mid-season, after just 16 months in the top job at The Hawthorns, to become once more, Vic Buckingham's assistant, this time at Sheffield Wednesday. In 1964, Clark again took the helm himself, this time at Peterborough United, where he stayed for three years, long enough to take his Third Division side back to The Hawthorns for the two-legged semi-final of the Football League Cup, in 1965-66. Albion, of course, were by then managed by the former Peterborough manager, Jimmy Hagan, and it was Albion who triumphed 6-3 on aggregate, and went on to beat West Ham in the final. After leaving Peterborough, Clark went on to become assistant manager at Fulham, Philadelphia Furies in the NASL, and Queens Park Rangers.

COACHES. Albion's first official coach was Albert Evans, a former Aston Villa star, who took the job after his playing career had been abruptly ended by injury in 1910. The position of coach at The Hawthorns was usually taken by a former Albion player, with Jesse Pennington (until his business interests grew too extensive), Tommy Glidden and W.G. Richardson (from 1946 to his death in 1959) prominent servants of the club. In more recent years, ex-Walsall defender Albert McPherson did a great job for nearly 20 years, until ousted by Johnny Giles in favour of Nobby Stiles, in 1984. In 1983, manager Ron Wylie brought in Mike Kelly as coach, but relations between Kelly and the senior players at the time fell to such a low ebb that Wylie was forced to resign in February 1984, when the Albion board demanded Kelly's dismissal. In 1988, Ron Atkinson actually paid the wages of new coach Stuart Pearson before the club eventually took him on in a full-time coaching capacity, only for Bobby Gould to dismiss him, in bizarre circumstances, during the 1991-92 season, after the former Hull and Manchester United forward had been Albion's caretaker manager for nearly seven weeks following Brian Talbot's dismissal in January 1991. Currently, assistant manager Arthur Mann and former Albion midfielder John Trewick help manager Alan Buckley with day-to-day coaching of the first team.

COLOURS. Albion's famous navy blue and white striped shirts were first adopted in September 1885, and Albion have played in those colours ever since, with the exception of a few months in 1889, when a red and blue striped shirt with black shorts was tried out, unsuccessfully, and throughout most of World War Two, when the material was not available for striped shirts. Indeed, the side only managed to keep itself fitted out with plain navy blue jerseys by means of regular appeals in the club programme for clothing vouchers from supporters. The classic striped shirts returned to The Hawthorns on Boxing Day 1946, for the visit of Second Division leaders Newcastle United, after an absence of over six years. Since then, the basic striped design has remained, although details, such as the width of the stripes, and the colours of the sleeves (striped or white) has altered at intervals. Perhaps the greatest variation in design was for the 1992-3-4 seasons, when Albion played in what became known as the 'barcode' shirts – a pattern of alternating narrow and wide stripes similar to those found on barcodes on supermarket shelves. The latest variation, in the 1995-96 season, sees a return to strong blue stripes and the use of the old West Bromwich town coat of arms, not seen on Albion shirts since the '50s.

COMEBACKS. The most dramatic comeback by an Albion side in a single game in the club's history was undoubtedly that in the Lord Mayor of Birmingham's Charity Cup game at home to Small Heath (now Birmingham City) in September 1897. At one stage, Albion were 4-1 down, but came back magnificently to level at 4-4, to force extra-time, during which period they scored a further three goals to win an amazing game 7-4, Ben Garfield scoring four of the goals. In October 1887, in a friendly at Blackburn

Rovers, the boot was on the other foot. Four goals ahead in the first five minutes (George Askin completing the fastest hat-trick scored by an Albion player from the start of the game), Albion were five goals to the good 18 minutes into the game. By the 80th minute, incredibly, Albion were 6-5 down – but there was more drama to come, as Albion equalised with an own goal, then conceded a winner 30 seconds from time to lose 7-6! In recent memory, Albion supporters will recall a tremendous comeback against local rivals Aston Villa, who were leading 1-0 at The Hawthorns in January 1983, when a blitz in the last four minutes by Garry Thompson (2) and Cyrille Regis saw Albion win 3-1 against a shell-shocked Villa side. Over two legs of Cup competitions, Albion's best comeback was in the League Cup later that same year, after they lost the first leg of a first round game by three clear goals at Millwall – a splendid 5-1 home win saw the Third Division side beaten 5-4 on aggregate. Six years later, Albion lost 3-1 in the first leg of a second round League Cup tie at home to Bradford City, only to win the return 5-3, after extra time, and go through on away goals after a 6-6 aggregate draw. Probably the most controversial comebacks staged against the Albion were the League Cup final against Queens Park Rangers at Wembley in 1967 (Albion led 2-0 at half-time), which ultimately saw the departure of both full-back Bobby Cram and manager Jimmy Hagan and the 3-2 home defeat against Swansea City in January 1992 (Albion conceded three goals in the last 12 minutes) which precipitated the first demonstrations against manager Bobby Gould and chairman John Silk which saw both men ousted at the season's end.

COOKSON, JIMMY. Manchester-born Cookson was a prodigious goalscorer. Rejected as a youngster by Manchester City, Cookson eventually signed for Third Division North Chesterfield, and he was that Division's top scorer. By the time Albion signed the 22-year-old in June 1927, he had already scored 85 League goals for Chesterfield. He scored his 100th League goal whilst playing for Albion against South Shields in December 1927 – in only his 89th League game – the fastest first 100 League goals in the history of the Football League, a record which will almost certainly never be beaten. Cookson started off his Albion career in a similarly explosive fashion, scoring on his debut in a 3-1 defeat at Oldham in the

Jimmy Cookson

opening game of the 1927-28 season. He then went on to score ten goals in his first six games, the high point being the game against Blackpool at The Hawthorns on 17 September 1927, when he created a new club record by becoming the first Albion player to score six goals in a League game, beating Freddy Morris's five-goal record from 1919. At the end of that first season, Cookson had scored another new record of 38 League goals, at exactly a goal a game and although he was out with injury for a good part of the following campaign, he still managed another 21 goals in 31 League games, plus another seven goals in the FA Cup. The 1929-30 season was a particularly good one for the Albion forwards, as they set a new club record of 105 League goals in 42 games – and Jimmy Cookson hit 34 of that total, in just 33 games. In the last four games alone, when the Albion hit 19 goals in wins against Hull (7-1), Spurs (4-3), Stoke (3-0) and Southampton (5-1), Cookson hit the net 11 times. Albion got off to a great start in the 1930-31 season, and Cookson was amongst the goals again, with 11 in the first 16 games, but, even with that scoring record, he lost his place to another, more skilful young centre-forward, W.G. Richardson. Cookson's record for the Albion was an amazing 110 goals in 131 appearances – none of the goals coming in the First Division – and he went on to score another 80 or so goals for first Plymouth and then Swindon before his retirement to become a publican in the Wiltshire town in 1938, so increasing his career record to 255 League goals in only 290 games. His amazing goal-scoring had continued in his 'wasted years' at The Hawthorns from 1931-33, when he managed to score a further 95 goals in reserve team football, which, at that time, was at least equal to the standard of the Third Division. Jimmy Cookson comes into the Albion story once more, in 1944, when he recommended a young Swindon-born inside-forward, who was playing for the works side of the Swindon-based record turntable manufacturers, Garrards, to the Albion. His name? The great Ray Barlow, who went on to play nearly 500 games for the Baggies.

CRAM, BOBBY. Bobby Cram (uncle of distance runner Steve Cram) was a Durham-born right-back who came up through the Albion youth policy to spend 12 years at The Hawthorns, receiving a testimonial game against an All-Star Albion XI in May 1967. That game was his last appearance in an Albion shirt, for he was given a free transfer soon after, mainly as a result of Albion's shock defeat against Third Division Queens Park Rangers – his last competitive Albion game – in the League Cup final two months before. Cram had played nearly 200 games for the club, scoring over 30 goals, mostly from the penalty spot. In September 1964, he became only the second Albion defender (after Sid Bowser) to score a hat-trick in a League game, when he scored three goals (two penalties) in a 5-3 win against Stoke City at The Hawthorns. Cram was kept out of the right-back position by England international Don Howe, but once Howe moved to Arsenal in 1964, Cram made the position his own, although he had also managed to get into the side at right-half and, for a five-match spell, at centre-forward (two goals). After three years in Canada with Vancouver Royals and Vancouver All Stars (with whom he played against the Albion in the 1969 tour of Canada), Cram returned to English football with Colchester United, and he, along with another former Baggie, Ray Crawford, was in their side that shocked mighty Leeds United in the 1971 FA Cup. Six months later, Bobby Cram returned to The Hawthorns for the last time, to captain Fourth Division Colchester to a famous penalty shoot-out victory in the Watney Cup final, after the two sides had drawn 4-4 after extra time.

CUNNINGHAM, LAURIE. Laurie Cunningham was perhaps the most gifted player ever to wear Albion's blue and white stripes. Fast, skilful and confident, he broke into the big time after starting his career with little Leyton Orient, Johnny Giles bringing him from Brisbane Road to The Hawthorns in a deal which saw both Joe Mayo and Allan Glover going in the opposite direction in a deal worth £110,000. That was in March 1977, and his skill revitalised the side and saw them go close to clinching a late place in the UEFA Cup, as he scored six goals in his 13 games that season. Cunningham only played another 73 League games for the Albion – two full seasons – but they were two of the best seasons in the club's history. In 1978 he helped take the side to an FA Cup semi-final against Ipswich then, in 1979, the club finished third in the First Division (its best placing for a quarter of a century) and reached the quarter-final of the UEFA Cup. Throughout that two-year period, Cunningham was undoubtedly the best winger in England, a fact which was recognised in 1977 when he became the first black player to be capped at any level for England (Under-21 versus Scotland at Bramall Lane). Cunningham was just pipped by Forest's Viv Anderson for the distinction of becoming the full England side's first black player, but he did go on to win six full England caps, although he never reproduced his club form at international level. In June 1979, Cunningham became one of the first players to take advantage of the new freedom of contract laws, when he signed for crack Spanish side Real Madrid in a £995,000 deal. Although he had several injury problems during his time in Spain (and was loaned out to Sporting Gijon for a time) he still won Spanish League and Cup medals in 1980, and was in the Madrid side that lost to Liverpool in the 1981 European Cup final. After eight years on the Continent, with such clubs as Olympique Marseille, RSC Charleroi and FC Betis, Cunningham returned to England with Manchester United (on loan, teaming up with former manager Ron Atkinson) where he turned down a chance to play in the 1983 FA Cup final because of an injury doubt, Leicester City (with whom he made his last visit to The Hawthorns) and Wimbledon (with whom he won an FA Cup winners medal as a substitute at Wembley in 1988). After Wimbledon, Cunningham returned to Spain to play for Second Division Rayo Vallecano only to die in a car accident near Madrid in July 1989.

CZECHOSLOVAKIA. Albion have played two sides from the now defunct Czechoslovakia. During the Second World War, on 1 November 1941, Albion entertained a Czech Army side at The Hawthorns, winning 3-1 in front of just 2,638 spectators. In May 1969, in an end of season tournament in Palo Alto, California, Albion beat top Czech side Dukla Prague 2-1 in their first game in the competition, Dick Krzywicki scoring both of Albion's goals.

D

DAVIES, STAN. Albion got off to a poor start at the beginning of the 1921-22 season, failing to score in nine of the club's first 14 League games, and slumping into the relegation area of the First Division, just a year after winning their first ever League Championship. Normally reliable centre-forward Freddie Morris did not score in the first 16 games, so the club had to look elsewhere for goals, so they signed Welsh international forward Stanley Davies, from Everton, for a sizeable £3,300 fee. Davies made his Albion debut in a 2-0 home win against Manchester City on 26 November 1921, the week after a 6-1 defeat at City's Hyde Road ground had sent Albion to the bottom of the First Division. Albion never looked back, quickly rising up the table to a final position of 13th, helped significantly by Davies' haul of 14 goals in 25 games, a record which made him Albion's top scorer for the season. A versatile forward, Davies played most of his six years at the Albion as a centre-forward, finishing as top scorer again in 1922-23, with 20 goals, and 1925-26 (19 goals) although he did also play a few games at centre-half, right-wing and inside-left and right, his last game coming in the Albion's final First Division game before relegation in May 1927, when he scored in a 2-2 draw with Manchester United. After an Albion career in which he scored 77 League goals in 147 games, Davies moved to Birmingham for one season (two goals in 14 games in 1927-28) having a short spell as player-manager at Cardiff City before finishing his League career at Barnsley in 1930.

DEBUTS, SCORING. It is a far from rare occurrence for players, particularly forwards, to score in their first Albion appearance; recent players to do just that include Andy Hunt, John Paskin, Andy Gray, Cyrille Regis and Bob Taylor. Less so for midfielders, but Craig Shakespeare, Robert Hopkins and Tony Morley have all done so fairly recently. Much rarer is the defender who scores on his debut, the most feted being 17-year-old Derek Statham when he scored a truly magnificent goal – past England keeper Peter Shilton – on his debut against Stoke City at the Victoria Ground in December 1976. Three Albion men have scored hat-tricks (or better) in their first appearance in an Albion shirt. In September 1913, centre-forward Alf Bentley scored all four goals in a 4-1 home win over Burnley, whilst William Jordan (against Gainsborough Trinity in 1907) and Albert Lewis (against Burnley, away, in 1904) both scored three goals on their debut. In 1996, Dutchman Richard Sneekes scored in his first three games for the Albion – the first midfield player to do so.

DEFEATS, FEWEST. The fewest number of League defeats suffered by Albion in a season is just four, when Albion won the Second Division at the first attempt in 1901-02. That was from a total of 34 League games; the fewest number of defeats in a 42-match programme, as most of Albion's seasons in the League have been, was seven, in 1978-79, which also set a new record for the fewest defeats away from home – four. The 1901-02 season also saw Albion's best home record, with just one defeat in 17 games at The Hawthorns. Since 1986, Albion have always played 46 games per season, and their best record was in the Second Division in 1988-89, when they lost just ten games. Albion's best undefeated run came in that 1901-02 Second Division Championship season, when, between December 1901 and March 1902, they played 17 League games without defeat. The run was equalled in 1957-58, when Albion played 17 unbeaten League games between September and December 1957. On the latter occasion, though, there was no FA Cup defeat in the middle of the sequence, as there had been in 1902. Albion's best run without defeat in the FA Cup (obviously, straddling one of their wins in the competition, was from January 1968 to March 1969, when they played 14 Cup ties without loss.)

DEFEATS, MOST. Albion's relegation season from the First Division in 1985-86 was a real record-breaker – for all the wrong reasons. The side lost a club record 26 games (from 42 matches), including a new record of ten home defeats, and also set another new record of losing nine games in a row.

DEFEATS, SUCCESSIVE. For 83 years Albion's record run of consecutive League defeats was eight, set in 1902-03. That was broken in 1985-6 when, after drawing the first game of the season at home to Oxford United, Albion lost their next nine League games. They were relegated from the First Division at the end of that season. Even that terrible record was beaten, comprehensively, in January 1996, when the side suffered its eleventh consecutive League defeat, a 3-1 loss at Port Vale on Boxing Day. Eleven days later, the FA Cup third round defeat at Crewe made it a round dozen losses in domestic competition. It should be noted that in this awful spell, between 28 October (lost 2-1 at Millwall) and 13 January (finally broke the losing run with a home 0-0 draw against Wolves), Albion did actually win two games, both in the Anglo-Italian Cup, against Reggiana and Brescia, so the worst spell of defeats in competitive first team games was actually six.

DEFEATS, WORST. Albion's worst defeat in the Football League came on 4 February 1937, when they lost 10-3 to Stoke City at the Victoria Ground, which beat the record set just two years before, when they had conceded nine goals for the first time in a 9-3 loss against Derby at the Baseball Ground. In 1955, rookie keeper Reg Davies became the second Albion custodian to let in ten when a virtually full-strength side lost 10-5 in a testimonial at Southern League Hereford United; including that game, Davies' record in goal in his Albion first team career was: played five, conceded 24! Albion's worst home defeat in first-class competition is 6-1, which was inflicted on the Albion in their first season at The Hawthorns, by Nottingham Forest who, coincidentally, Albion had beaten 8-0 in their final game at Stoney Lane just five home games earlier! Thirty-six years later, Sunderland also won 6-1 at The Hawthorns, in Albion's relegation season of 1936-37. Only two other sides have scored as many as six goals in a League game in West Bromwich; Aston Villa, who won 6-3 at Stoney Lane in October 1893 and, most recently, Everton, who won 6-2 at The Hawthorns in March 1968. Nine weeks later, Albion beat the same Everton side 1-0 in the FA Cup final at Wembley. Albion's worst defeat in the FA Cup took place as recently as February 1967, when they lost 5-0 to an outstanding Leeds United side in the fourth round tie at Elland Road. At home, their lowest point in the FA Cup was reached in January 1905, when they lost 5-2 to Leicester Fosse in what was the intermediate round of the Cup.

In the League Cup, the Albion's worst defeat was at the City Ground in October 1982, when Ron Wylie's side unexpectedly lost 6-1 to League Cup specialists Nottingham Forest; Albion won the second leg of the tie, to go out 7-4 on aggregate. At home, only one side has scored as many as four goals against the Albion in a League Cup tie; Reading, who won 4-2 at The Hawthorns in October 1995 (5-3 on aggregate), although Fourth Division Peterborough United did win 3-0 there in August 1988. Albion's worst ever home defeat in any competition, i.e. including the many local cup tournaments that Albion used to enter in the first thirty years of their existence, was a 0-7 loss at the hands of Wolverhampton Wanderers in the Birmingham Senior Cup in January 1899.

DEFENSIVE RECORDS, BEST. The best season in Albion's history, defensively speaking, was in their unsuccessful Second Division promotion campaign of 1908-09, when they conceded just 27 goals in 38 games, or around 0.71 goals per game. In a 42-game season (1919-86), the best record was in 1924-25, when Albion finished as runners-up in the First Division – 34 goals conceded. Since their decline in the mid-'80s, Albion have been playing 46 games a season in either Division Two or Three (old style) and their best record in that number of games is 41 goals conceded in 1988-89. For an individual goalkeeper, the Albion record of 'clean sheets' by a custodian belongs to John Osborne, who played in every game in the 1975-76 promotion season, and kept a clean sheet on a record 22 occasions in 42 games.

DEFENSIVE RECORDS, WORST. Albion sides have never conceded a century of League goals in a season, but they went close in their First Division season of 1936-37, when they were just two goals short of the 'ton'. Of course, ten of those goals came in one game, the club's record League defeat of 10-3, at Stoke's Victoria Ground. Nearly as bad was the relegation season, the following year, when 91 goals were conceded, including seven in one game at Maine Road, and another six at home to Sunderland. The only other season where as many as 90 goals have been conceded was 1954-55, when defensive instability was the reason for such a rapid decline after the achievements of the previous season; 96 goals were let through, with Leicester, in particular, scoring ten goals against the Baggies in their two League games.

DONOVAN, KEVIN. Kevin Donovan was plucked by Albion's assistant manager, Keith Burkinshaw, from the obscurity of Huddersfield Town's reserve side to play a vital role in Albion's 1992-93 Second Division promotion campaign under Ossie

Kevin Donovan

Ardiles. Although he scored only seven goals in his 33 games that season, his last goal of the campaign was the clincher at Wembley in the play-off final against Port Vale. His selection for the number 11 shirt had solved a problem in the side which Ardiles had attempted to fill with Gary Robson, Luther Blissett, Kwame Ampadu and Alan Dickens, before settling on the Halifax-born youngster. Since then, Donovan has often impressed in the side, but has yet to realise his true potential – on form, he can be unplayable as a winger, but has lacked consistency in what has usually been a struggling Albion side.

DOUBLE, THE. Albion nearly won the ultimate prize in English domestic football – the 'Double' of the First Division Championship and the FA Cup – in 1954. Dubbed 'The Team of the Century', Albion's precision passing and prolific goalscoring kept them at the top of the First Division for almost the whole of the 1953-54 season, and they were favourites to become the first team of the 20th century to achieve the Double – which, up to then, had only been managed by Preston North End, in 1889 and Aston Villa, in 1897. There were so many more games played in modern times, and at a much higher standard, that the Double was felt to be an impossible target, and indeed, although Albion managed to win the FA Cup, beating Preston 3-2 at Wembley, their League title chase faltered badly. In top position almost uninterruptedly from the start of the season, they were top, with 50 points, when they travelled to Roker Park to play Sunderland four days after their successful FA Cup semi-final against Port Vale. However, international selections (Ronnie Allen and Johnny Nicholls, for England's game on the following Saturday) meant that Albion had to field an understrength side in the midweek game, playing coach Freddy Cox at centre-forward, alongside inexperienced reserve, Wilf Carter. Relegation-haunted Sunderland won 2-1, after Albion had lost goalkeeper Norman Heath (the injury ended his football career) and had centre-half Kennedy on the wing, suffering from concussion. Ray Barlow won a standing ovation for his makeshift performance in the Albion goal, but had no chance with the winning goal, scored just four minutes from time. On the Saturday, as luck would have it, Albion had to meet second placed Wolves, who were two points behind, with six games remaining, still without Allen and

Nicholls, playing for England against Scotland at Hampden. Wolves had Wright and Mullen missing, but with their greater squad size they were barely missed as Wolves won 1-0, after Barlow, playing this time at centre-forward, was put out of the game in the first ten minutes by Wolves' notorious hardman, Bill Shorthouse. Their confidence gone, Albion won just one of their last seven games, to end up as runners-up, four points adrift of the Wolves. Twenty-three years previously, though, Albion won another 'Double' on which they still have a unique hold, when they became the only club, so far, ever to win the FA Cup and promotion from the Second Division in the same season. On that occasion, they finished well behind Champions Everton in the League, so went up only as runners-up, but beat First Division Birmingham City 2-1 at Wembley, with W.G. Richardson scoring both Albion goals. Five days after the win at Wembley, with their promotion place by no means assured, the side won 1-0 at Stoke, Richardson again scoring the only goal, then clinched promotion on the last day of the season with a thrilling 3-2 win over Charlton Athletic, in front of 52,415 spectators at The Hawthorns – and 'W.G.' once more scored the winning goal!

DUDLEY, JIMMY. Although born in Scotland, Jimmy Dudley was brought up from a very early age in West Bromwich. His brother, George, played for the Albion's first team just before World War Two, when he became the first Scot to play for the Albion for over 30 years. He was also a cousin of another former Albion stalwart, Jimmy Edwards. It was only natural, then, that young Jimmy should sign professional for the Albion at the end of the war, although it took him over four years to make it into the first team, at right-half in a 1-1 draw in the First Division at Maine Road in December 1950. A superbly creative right-half, it took Jimmy just two years to make the number four shirt his own, taking over from Joe Kennedy, who switched to an equally successful career as a centre-half. Dudley's must have been the first name pencilled in on the team-sheet, for from 5 April 1952 to 3 March 1956, he set a new club record by appearing in 166 consecutive League games, a record which he held until broken first by Tony Godden, then Alistair Robertson, in the early '80s. Dudley, surprisingly, was only capped at 'B' level by Scotland, at a time when 'Anglos' were not favoured in the full international side. He played over 300 games for the Albion, scoring 11 times, the most important goal undoubtedly being the rather fortunate equaliser against little Port Vale in the 1954 FA Cup semi-final at Villa Park. He played his last Albion game in a 4-1 defeat at West Ham in September 1959, moving on to Walsall for £4,000 in December of that year, helping them, over nearly 200 games, to promotion from the Fourth and Third Divisions in successive seasons, 1959-60 and 1960-61, finally retiring from the game in 1966.

E

ECWC. Albion's only foray into the European Cup Winners Cup came in the 1968-69 season, after they achieved qualification by winning the FA Cup final. The side reached the quarter-final stage by beating RFC Bruges on the away goals rule (3-3 on aggregate) and Dinamo Bucharest (5-1). They lost by a single goal to Scottish Cup holders Dunfermline Athletic, after getting a goalless draw in the first leg in Scotland.

ELLIOTT, BILLY. Cumbrian-born William Elliott could have chosen between football and rugby as a professional career, eventually signing as a 17-year-old for Carlisle United, despite the interest of Rugby League side Swinton. A year on the ground staff at Wolverhampton Wanderers followed, under the notorious Major Buckley, but Wolves soon lost interest and the winger signed for Bournemouth early in 1938. On 22 December of that year, Fred Everiss travelled down to the south coast club, and signed young Elliott for £4,000, putting him straight in Albion's promotion-seeking Second Division side at Kenilworth Road, Luton, on Christmas Eve – a 3-1 defeat. Elliott scored his first Albion goal in his next game, another defeat, at Swansea, ending the season with three goals in 17 games, as Albion slipped out of the promotion race because of a serious shortage of goals, with Elliott having the worst spell of his Albion career. By October

1939, Elliott was in barracks in the South Staffs regiment, playing very occasionally for the Albion at 30 shillings a game. By 1941, however, he was a regular fixture in Albion's Football League South side, scoring 31 goals from the right wing before being posted abroad to Italy during 1944-45. By the start of the 1945-46 'transitional' season, Elliott was back in the Albion side and scored 19 goals in 34 appearances, a remarkable total for a wide player, making him joint top scorer with Ike Clarke. It was at that time that Elliott won his two Wartime Victory International caps for England, both awarded to him because the man that all right wingers of the time had to understudy, Stanley Matthews, had had to withdraw from the England side through injury. Elliott was Albion's first choice winger for the next three and a half seasons, during which he added a further 180 League and Cup games to his 150 wartime appearances for the club, providing innumerable goals for his fellow forwards, Dave Walsh, Ike Clarke and Jack Haines. By his own admission, Billy Elliott was a 'one-trick' man, where he used his deceptive drag back to momentarily fool opposing full-backs before beating them comprehensively with an awesome burst of speed. A great servant for the Albion until he seriously injured his Achilles tendon on Christmas Eve 1949, in a First Division game at home to Manchester United. He attempted a comeback over the first dozen or so games of the following season, but after another poor showing in the home defeat against Tottenham Hotspur in October 1950, he notified Albion secretary Eph Smith that he intended to retire from professional football at the end of the season. His time at the Albion ended the following July, and he then had a spell as player-manager with Bilston Town before becoming a publican, later assisting in the formation of the first West Bromwich Albion Supporters Club.

EVERISS, ALAN. Alan, like his father, joined the club as a lowly-paid office boy in 1933. In 1960 he took over as Albion club secretary upon the retirement of Eph Smith, and held the post until stepping down in 1980, when, like his father, he became a director of the club, until he left the board in 1986. He is still a life member of the Albion, so the Everiss connection still remains unbroken – 100 years from 1896 to the present day.

EVERISS, FRED. Fred Everiss' contribution to the history of West

Bromwich Albion was immense. West Bromwich-born Fred was appointed as office boy shortly after leaving school, in 1896, and was appointed club secretary in 1902. In those days, the job was not merely an administrative one, as it is now, but also covered the matchday duties now down to the team manager; the team may have been chosen by the directors at that time, but before, during and after the game itself, Fred Everiss was in charge. In his time in office, Albion won promotion from the Second Division in 1911 (as Champions) and 1931 (as runners-up) and won the Football League Championship in 1920 and the FA Cup in 1931. Fred remained as Albion secretary for 46 years, until the manager-secretary job was finally split, as it had been long before at other clubs, into two posts, with Jack Smith coming in as manager and Ephraim Smith – Everiss' brother-in-law, and his assistant for 37 years! – taking over as secretary on Fred's retirement. Everiss was made a club director, which he kept until his death in 1951.

F

FA CUP. The Albion are currently in their worst ever spell in the FA Cup; since 1984, they have won just six out of their last 22 FA Cup games. Things were so very different before that, for Albion have to be considered one of the finest cup-fighting sides in the history of the competition to that point. They first entered the competition in its 13th season – and Albion's sixth – but lost 2-0 at home to Wednesbury Town in the first round. Amazingly, two years later, they became the first Midlands side to reach the FA Cup final, where they did well to hold mighty Blackburn Rovers, who had won the trophy two years running, to a goalless draw at the Oval. Rovers won the replay at 2-0; no side has won the Cup three years running since. Albion reached the final again the following year (lost to Aston Villa) and again in 1888, when they won the Cup for the first time, and they won it again in 1892, 1931, 1954 and 1968. In the period 1931-37, they reached two finals, plus a losing semi-final, against Preston, at Highbury in 1937. In 1969, as holders, they lost to a goal from Leicester City's Allan Clarke four minutes from the end of another semi-final. Albion reached the semi-final stage in both 1978 and 1982, but gave very disappointing performances, at Highbury again, on each occasion, when they lost to Ipswich Town and Queens Park Rangers. The low point of Albion's FA Cup history undoubtedly came on 5 January 1991, when they lost 4-2 at home to Diadora side

Woking, although two years later, again as an (old) Second Division club, they again lost to a non-League side, Halifax Town, in a first round tie.

FA CUP FINALS. Albion have reached the FA Cup final on ten occasions, winning the trophy five times. The last time was as long ago as 1968 – but Coventry City are still the only other side from the Midlands to get to the final since then. When Albion won in 1888, they were the first side to do so with an all-English side; in fact, eight of the side were actually born in West Bromwich itself, with the exceptions, Aldridge (Walsall), Bayliss (Tipton) and Wilson (Handsworth), all born within five miles of the town. Remarkably, when they won the Cup in 1931, it was again with an all-English side.

1886	Blackburn Rovers 0-2 (at Derby CCC) after a 0-0 draw at The Oval
1887	Aston Villa 0-2 (The Oval)
1888	Preston NE 2-1 (The Oval)
1892	Aston Villa 3-0 (The Oval)
1895	Aston Villa 0-1 (The Oval)
1912	Barnsley 0-1 (Sheffield) after a 0-0 draw at Crystal Palace
1931	Birmingham 2-1 (Wembley)
1935	Sheffield Wednesday 2-4 (Wembley)
1954	Preston NE 3-2 (Wembley)
1968	Everton 1-0 (aet) (Wembley)

Albion and Aston Villa have met on three occasions in the FA Cup final (plus once at the semi-final stage); no other two clubs have met as many times at such an advanced stage of the competition.

FA CUP, GOALS. The most goals scored by an Albion player in an FA Cup run is ten, by Jem Bayliss in 1887-88. In total, Bayliss scored 24 FA Cup goals during his Albion career, a total later bettered only by W.G. Richardson and Tony Brown, who both managed 26. Only one Albion player has scored in every round of the competition; Jeff Astle, who scored nine goals in the six rounds (nine games) of Albion's 1967-68 Cup-winning season.

FA Cup Winners - 1968

FA CUP SEMI-FINALS. Albion have reached the FA Cup semi-final on 19 occasions: in 1886, 1887, 1888, 1889, 1891, 1892, 1895, 1901, 1907, 1912, 1931, 1935, 1937, 1954, 1957, 1968, 1969, 1978 and 1982. They won ten of the 19 ties. The longest semi-final tie was against Nottingham Forest, in 1892, when the Albion needed three games to reach the final, eventually winning 6-2 in a snowstorm at Derby.

FA CUP SEMI-FINALS, AT THE HAWTHORNS. Twice the Albion have staged FA Cup semi-finals at The Hawthorns. In March 1902, Derby County and Sheffield United drew 1-1, in front of 33,603 spectators. Fifty-eight years later, in March 1960, Wolves beat Aston Villa 1-0 but this time the attendance had grown to 55,596.

FAIRS CUP. The Albion first qualified for European competition in 1966-67, by virtue of winning the Football League Cup the previous season. They took part in the Inter-Cities Fairs Cup, a forerunner of the UEFA Cup, and beat DOS Utrecht 6-3 on aggregate in their first ever European tie. Unfortunately, they lost 6-1 on aggregate to Bologna in the next round. Their League placing of ninth in 1968 would also have been enough to grant them entry into the Fairs Cup, but they won the FA Cup and thus played in the ECWC. Newcastle United took their place in the Fairs Cup – and won the trophy in 1969!

FANZINES. The 'fanzine phenomenon' started in the mid-'80s, and West Bromwich Albion supporters, along with those of Bradford City and York, were in the vanguard of the movement, with the launch of the *Fingerpost* magazine in 1984. Originally the in-house magazine of the Halesowen Branch of the Albion Supporters Club, the *Fingerpost* developed, by 1988, into a professionally produced, glossy A5 magazine selling over 2,000 copies, eventually folding after disputes with the parent club, in 1990. It was replaced by three fanzines, the hopeless *Albion Chronicle*, the execrable and unmissed *Last Train to Rolfe Street*, now defunct, and the still-thriving *Grorty Dick*, which has reached its 50th issue.

FIRST GAME. For many years, the earliest reference to an Albion game was for the friendly against Black Lake Victoria on 13 December 1879, which was presumed to be the West Bromwich Strollers (as they were then known) first game. That was a 12-a-side match, won 1-0 by the Albion in front of around 500 spectators in Dartmouth Park. However, it was found recently that a team comprised of many of the regular founder-members of the Albion played another 12-a-side game on 23 November 1878, playing for a George Salter Spring Works side against another company team, Hudson's. With Bob Roberts, George Bell, Jim Stanton and John Stokes, this team was recognisably an Albion one, and this goalless draw may well be the oldest traceable Albion game. The Albion side that day was: R. Roberts, G. Bell, J. Stanton, J. Forrester, H. Evans, T. Waterfield, J. Siddons, J.S tokes, S. Evans, E. Evans, W. Jones, S. Jones.

FOOTBALL LEAGUE. Albion were founder members of the Football League in 1888. On 2 March of that year, William McGregor wrote to what he considered to be the top five clubs in

75

the country: Albion, Preston, Aston Villa, Bolton and Blackburn Rovers, detailing his plans for what he called 'the Association Football Union' involving the top dozen English clubs – as FA Cup holders, Albion were obviously prime candidates for any such move. The new competition was officially launched on 17 April and the first League games were played on 8 September 1888, Albion winning their first ever League game 2-0 at Stoke. At that point, the League had still not settled a points system for ordering the clubs, but by the end of November it was decided to award two points for a win and one for a draw (although Albion proposed at that meeting that points only be awarded for victories). As the only winning side to keep a clean sheet on that opening day of the Football League, Albion were technically the first-ever leaders of the Football League, on the basis of goal average! Albion eventually finished sixth, and were 18 points behind the unbeaten Champions Preston. Since then, Albion have never really shone in the League, winning the Championship just once, in 1920, and finishing as runners-up twice more, in 1925 and 1954.

FOOTBALL LEAGUE CUP. Although the Football League Cup got underway in 1960, it was shunned by many of the big clubs, including the Albion, who only entered the competition in 1965, when the winners (as long as they were a First Division club) were guaranteed entry into the Fairs Cup. Amazingly, Albion won the Cup at the first time of asking, beating West Ham United 5-3 in the two-legged final, and reached the final again the following year. This time the venue was Wembley, with a 100,000 crowd, and Albion reached possibly the nadir of their great history when they threw away a two-goal lead against Third Division Queens Park Rangers, to lose 3-2. Albion's record over their first five years in the competition was astonishing, and they reached Wembley again in 1970, when they lost 2-1 to Manchester City. They also reached the semi-final of the League Cup in 1982, when they lost 1-0 on aggregate to Tottenham. In recent years, their record in the competition, in whichever of its various sponsors' guises (Milk, Rumbelows, Littlewoods, Coca-Cola Cups) has been exceedingly poor. It took Albion just 12 games, and 13 months, to record their first ten wins in the new competition back in 1965, and they did not lose at The Hawthorns in their first six years in the League Cup. Their last ten victories took 39 games, over the last 13 years!

FOOTBALL LEAGUE CUP, FINALS. Albion have reached the final of the Football League Cup three times, winning the competition once, against West Ham in the last two-legged final in 1965-66.

FOOTBALL LEAGUE CUP, SEMI-FINALS. Albion have reached the penultimate stage of the League Cup on four occasions, only once failing to progress to the final, in 1981-82. All the semi-finals were two-legged affairs. The Hawthorns has also staged another League Cup semi-final, on 18 December 1968, when Swindon Town and Burnley, level on aggregate after the two legs of their semi-final, including extra time, played off their replay to see who would get to Wembley. Third Division Swindon Town won 3-2 and went on to emulate Queens Park Rangers' feat against the Albion two years earlier, by beating Arsenal 3-1 at Wembley.

FORMATION. For many years, it has been told that the Albion was formed, as West Bromwich Strollers, on 20 September 1879, by a group of young workmen from George Salter Springs in West Bromwich. A tale was told about a two-mile walk to neighbouring Wednesbury to buy the club's first football. Local newspapers record a Strollers game soon afterwards, but it has recently emerged that the Salters' side, with many of the players who were to become Strollers men, was playing as early as November 1878, when a game against Hudson's Works side was recorded – and this is now recognised as Albion's first recorded game. The result was a 0-0 draw.

FRANCE. Albion have only once played a French side in a public match, when they beat Caen 2-0 at The Hawthorns in January 1989. However, the Albion did play Auxerre behind closed doors at The Hawthorns in a private practice match in 1991, which the French side used as part of their preparations for their UEFA Cup tie with Liverpool. Albion won 2-1 – and Liverpool came back from a 2-0 deficit to beat the French side 3-2 on aggregate.

FRASER, DOUG. Dougie Fraser was a fearsome, tough-tackling wing-half who gave Albion great service during the '60s. Rejected after trials with Celtic and Leeds United in the '50s, Fraser made his name with some excellent performances for Aberdeen in the Scottish First Division. In September 1963, he was one of new manager Jimmy Hagan's first signings for the Albion, for a fee of £23,000, making his Albion debut in a 3-1 home win against Birmingham City on the 18th of that month. He was to keep his place, virtually continuously, right up to the end of the 1969-70 season, when he led the Albion side out, as captain, for the League Cup final against Manchester City at Wembley. Playing mostly at right- or left-half, but with occasional games at either right or left-back, the versatile defender eventually settled down to playing at right-back, recording over 300 games for the club, and, along with fellow defenders Graham Williams and John Kaye, making up one of the toughest defensive lines ever fielded by the club. He also won two international caps for Scotland during the '60s, against Cyprus and Holland, and appeared for Albion in all of their Cup finals during this period – 1966, 1967, 1968 and 1970. Fraser's last Albion game was as right-back in a 2-2 draw at home to Chelsea in November 1970, and he was sold by manager Alan Ashman to Nottingham Forest two months later for £35,000, returning to The Hawthorns as Forest's captain in March 1972 for a relegation decider (that Albion won 1-0). In July 1973, Fraser returned to the West Midlands as a player with Walsall, where he hit the headlines for being sent off for fighting in a match against Bristol Rovers – against his former Albion team-mate, Kenny Stephens! At the start of the 1974-75 season, Fraser was appointed Walsall manager, but retired from the game two years later to take up a career as a prison warder in Nottingham.

FRIENDLIES. For the first three seasons of the club's existence, 1878-81, the club could only play friendly games, until they were accepted into first the Birmingham County FA, and then the Staffordshire FA, when they became eligible to play in those Associations' County Cups. Entry into the FA Cup came in 1883, but, even so, the bulk of the club's finances still came from a full fixture list of friendlies. Early games in the club's history were exclusively against local sides, such as Black Lake Victoria,

Smethwick Trinity, Hockley Belmont, Oldbury and fellow West Bromwich sides, Rovers and Royal. Gradually, as the club's reputation grew, with its exploits in the local and national cups, matches were arranged with the bigger outfits in Lancashire, Yorkshire and Scotland, as Albion met Preston North End (1883), Blackburn Rovers (1883) and Olympic (1885), Third Lanark (1885) and Hibernian (1886). By 1888, Albion had reached the FA Cup final three times in succession, and apart from the 20 Cup ties they were involved in, they also managed to arrange another 35 friendly games with such clubs as Oxford and Cambridge Universities, Sheffield Wednesday, Third Lanark, Blackburn Rovers and Preston North End (three times, including two fixtures played after their epic FA Cup final meeting). The 1888-89 season saw the introduction of the first guaranteed fixture list of Football League games, which was eventually to kill off the friendly, apart from pre-season warm-up games, but even in 1888-89, Albion still arranged 29 friendlies, to add to a similar number of League and Cup games, to take full advantage of Albion's position as FA Cup holders. It was not until around 1905 that Albion effectively stopped playing friendlies – in the 1904-05 season, they played five such games, all away. In the following 50 years, excluding wartime, they played just seven more friendlies – and five of those were against famed amateur side Corinthians – who by their nature could only play in such non-competitive encounters. For a time, after the introduction of floodlights at The Hawthorns, Albion played a number of floodlight friendlies against continental opposition, including CDSA Moscow, Athletico Bilbao, a Bucharest XI, Grenchen of Switzerland and a Canadian Touring XI, but as the novelty of floodlit matches declined, so did the gates, dropping from 52,805 (v. CDSA in 1957) to 9,411 (Alkmaar of Holland in 1964). Changes in the Football Association regulations regarding the staging of pre-season friendlies in the late '60s saw the introduction of warm-up games against clubs from other divisions, which are now a regular feature for all clubs – before that, the warm-up games between first and second teams (whites against the stripes) were a regular feature of the pre-season at The Hawthorns. During the period of management of Ron Atkinson, 1978-81, the club played an enormous number of friendlies, testimonial games and foreign tour matches – as many as 15 in 1978-79 alone, to add to the 59 games in League, FA Cup, League Cup and the UEFA Cup.

FULL MEMBERS CUP. The Full Members Cup was established in 1985, for the First and Second Division clubs, to help compensate for the UEA ban on English clubs in Europe, but it never really gained any sort of popularity. In an otherwise truly miserable season, Albion reached the Southern Area semi-final, after disposing of Brighton (at the Goldstone Ground) and Crystal Palace (at home) in a round-robin competition, where they lost 5-4 on penalties (after a 2-2 draw) to Chelsea, the eventual first winners of the competition. The following season saw an attendance of less than a thousand at Albion's game at Millwall, in the final, unsponsored season of the Cup, which was renamed the Simod Cup for the 1987-88 season (*see* SIMOD CUP).

G

GALE, ARTHUR. Arthur Gale was one of Albion's most unjustly treated players. He signed from Chester in 1931 and played, mostly in Albion's all conquering Central League side of that time, until returning back to Sealand Road where he continued to combine football with his profession as a teacher. He had a phenomenal record as a goal scorer in the Albion reserve side, scoring 136 goals in 146 games, but rarely managed to displace W.G. Richardson in the first team. When Gale did make the first XI, he scored a creditable 12 goals in 29 games, but his cruellest season was 1934-35 when, as a stand-in on the right wing for Albion captain Tommy Glidden, he scored in every round of the Albion's FA Cup run as far as the semi-final, but was sensationally dropped for the Wembley final itself against Sheffield Wednesday in favour of Glidden, whose breakdown in the game cost Albion the Cup.

GEDDES, ALF. A speedy left winger, Alf 'Jasper' Geddes was a very popular player with the Albion supporters at Stoney Lane when he came up through the ranks at the club in 1891. He left for Clapham Rovers and then Millwall, but sensationally returned for Albion's last two games of the 1894-95 campaign, which Albion had to win to remain in the First Division. It was a great return, as Albion won both games, against Nottingham Forest (1-0) and Sheffield Wednesday (6-0), with Geddes scoring in both. At the end of that season, mission accomplished, Geddes returned to Millwall, to captain the Lions to two successive Southern League Championships.

GERMANY. Before the reunification of the Federal Republic of Germany, Albion never played a West German side. In 1979, they did meet East German side Carl Zeiss Jena in the first round of the UEFA Cup. They lost the first leg behind the Iron Curtain, 2-0 and then, with Ally Brown sent off on the stroke of half-time, they lost the home leg 2-1 (1-4 on aggregate).

GIBRALTAR. Albion have played one friendly game in the British Territory of Gibraltar, when they beat a Gibraltan Select XI 4-0 in March 1992. The game was only significant in that it marked the first time that a father and son had ever played for the club in the same game, when Jonathan Gould appeared in goal and his father, Albion manager Bobby Gould, came on as a second-half substitute.

GILES, JOHN. Johnny Giles had an outstanding career as a player with Manchester United and Leeds United, winning most of the honours that the game has to offer, including 60 caps for the Republic of Ireland. He appeared in a record eleven FA Cup semi-finals, gaining two winners' and two runners-up medals, as well as being on the winning side in two Fairs Cup and one League Cup final. A marvellous midfielder, his last game for the great Leeds side of the '70s was in the 1975 European Cup final in Paris, after which he took over as Albion's player-manager, a remarkable gamble for the Albion, as it was generally felt at that time that no one could both play and manage at the same time at the highest level. After a poor start which saw Albion in their lowest ever position, at the foot of the Second Division, results started to improve with the judicial purchase of two experienced Irishmen, Mick Martin and Paddy Mulligan, and promotion was achieved with a last-gasp win at Oldham in May 1976. Immediately, Giles handed in his resignation – he wanted more say in the day-to-day financial running of the club – but was persuaded to continue for another year, by which time he had established the Albion as a First Division club, just missing out on a European place. Giles continued to play in the First Division, and made a total of 88

John Giles

appearances (5 goals) for the Albion, his silky skills undiminished by the fact that he was nearly 37 when he played his last game for the club. After eight great years in the First Division, Albion were fading badly by the time Giles returned to the club in February 1984, accompanied by his 'A-Team' of Nobby Stiles and Norman Hunter, and it seemed a bad omen when, in his first game in charge, Third Division Plymouth won 1-0 in an FA Cup fifth round tie at The Hawthorns. However, Giles went on to secure Albion's First Division place at the end of the 1983-84 season, and managed a satisfactory position of 12th place the following year. However, Giles was responsible for selling crowd favourite Cyrille Regis in 1984 – when he also sold Albion's other superb centre-forward, Garry Thompson, and replaced the two of them with two mobile, but very small forwards, Imre Varadi and Garth Crooks, the team's form fell right away. Giles resigned from his post in October 1985, after a 3-0 defeat at Coventry City had produced Albion's worst ever run of consecutive defeats – nine. In between his two spells at The Hawthorns, Giles was player-manager of Shamrock Rovers and coach at Vancouver Whitecaps in Canada, and was also manager of the Republic of Ireland side from 1973 to 1980. He is now a successful businessman and journalist with the Express Group of newspapers.

GLIDDEN, TOM. Part of a famed right-wing partnership with England international inside-right Joe Carter, Tommy Glidden was associated with the Albion for 52 years until his death in 1974. He signed for the club in 1922 and played in nearly 500 games, including two FA Cup finals, until his retirement in 1936. He captained the club from the wing for many years, as one of the finest ball players of his time, although he never won full international honours. He took over as coach from 1936 to 1939, then returned to the club in 1951 as a director until 1974.

GODDEN, TONY. Many Albion supporters still rate Tony Godden as the best Albion goalkeeper ever – he was certainly a great shot-stopper, and much under-appreciated during his ten-year spell at the club. Godden was brought from non-League Ashford Town, making his Albion debut in a 2-0 win at Tottenham in March 1977 (sharing an Albion debut with Laurie Cunningham). After six games, during which the Albion were unbeaten, manager Giles rested the youngster in favour of the more experienced John Osborne, but at the start of the following season, under Ronnie Allen, Godden was first choice keeper – and how! He kept his place in the side for what was then a new club record of 180 League games in a row – from August 1977 to October 1981. Counting League Cup, FA Cup and European ties, his total in the side was actually 228 games – a remarkable achievement, and testimony to the consistency that he brought to his game. Throughout his time at the club, Godden was criticised for failing to command his area, and for being weak in handling crosses – and few will forget his famous gaffe in 1978, when he allowed Liverpool's Kenny Dalglish to take the ball off him to score when he was rolling the ball in his area. After a long spell in the reserves, during which time he was replaced in the Albion goal by Mark Grew and Paul Barron, Godden regained his place with

Tony Godden

the return of Johnny Giles in 1984, only to lose it again to Ron Saunders' first signing, Stuart Naylor. Godden only played one game under Saunders – his final one for the Albion – a 5-0 defeat against Tottenham at White Hart Lane, the scene of his Albion debut nine years before. Godden's last game in an Albion shirt was against an Albion 1978 XI, in his own testimonial at The Hawthorns in May 1986. At the time, he was actually on loan to Chelsea, and he transferred to Stamford Bridge at the end of the season, finishing his League career with Bury, Birmingham City and Peterborough United, before going on to manage, amongst other non-League sides, Kings Lynn.

GOODMAN, DON. Leeds-born Goodman signed for Bradford City in July 1983 and won a Third Division Championship medal with them in 1985. He was deeply affected by the Bradford Fire

Don Goodman

Disaster, because his girlfriend was killed in the conflagration. After losing his place in the Bradford side, he was signed by Albion manager Ron Saunders on the transfer deadline day in March 1987, making his debut at Oldham in a 2-1 defeat. He played in ten games before the end of that season, scoring his first goal in a 1-1 draw at Crystal Palace, and helping Albion to retain their place in Division Two. The following season, under Ron Atkinson, Goodman was a regular in the side, but still only managed to score seven goals in 40 games. He was also very unpredictable, and in one mid-season trip to Portugal, Goodman got involved in a bar brawl with team-mate Tony Kelly. Goodman had excellent ball control, and amazing speed off the mark, but he was never a natural goalscorer, and he wasted an unbelievable number of goalscoring opportunities in his first two years at the club.

Then Atkinson introduced Stuart Pearson as a coach at the club, and, as a former prolific goal-scoring forward with Hull City and Manchester United, he spent a considerable amount of time and effort on Goodman. The results were plain for all to see at the start of the 1988-89 season, when the forward's play seemed transformed, with his 12 goals in 17 games helping the Albion to a place at the top of the Second Division table by Christmas 1988. Unfortunately, so great was the reliance that Albion placed on Goodman, that when he was 'crocked' in the FA Cup replay against Everton at Goodison Park, their season began to decline badly. With Goodman in and out of the side from then on, with persistent injuries, they slumped to a final finish just outside the play-offs. Fit again for 1989-90, Goodman flourished, whilst the Albion struggled. He scored a magnificent 21 goals in 39 League games, behind only Mick Quinn, Steve Bull and Guy Whittingham in the Second Division's top scorers; yet Albion only managed to avoid relegation in the penultimate game of the season. The following year, they were not so fortunate, and it was once again down to Goodman's absence that they struggled. Injured after coming on as a substitute at Hull in September 1990, Goodman made just one more full appearance before the end of March. Fit again for the relegation dog-fight under Bobby Gould, he scored five goals in eight starts during April, but, crucially, pulled a hamstring shortly after scoring a brilliant free-kick goal at home to Newcastle on 4 May. Albion were lucky to draw that game, and went to Twerton Park the following Saturday needing to win to be sure of avoiding relegation to the Third Division. With the inexperienced youngster Adrian Foster in Goodman's place, Albion lacked any punch and drew 1-1, and were relegated. Hit by injury again at the start of the following season, Goodman's seven goals in 11 games took Albion to the top of the Third Division, before the Albion directors decided to sell him to Sunderland for £900,000, against the wishes of manager Gould, in December 1991, shortly before Albion's FA Cup tie at Orient. They lost that and slumped down the table, until Bob Taylor was signed as a goal-scoring replacement the following February, too late, though, to win a play-off place. The sale of Goodman was one of several factors which instigated the supporters demonstrations staged at The Hawthorns throughout the tail-end of that season. Once he had left the Albion, Goodman's persistent injury problems seemed to clear up, and he hardly missed a game for the Roker Park club, as he forged a good striking partnership with Phil Gray to keep Sunderland in the Second Division, although having played for the Albion in their first round FA Cup tie against Marlow, he was Cup-tied and ineligible for Sunderland's 1992 FA Cup final appearance against Liverpool. In 1994, Goodman was signed by Graham Taylor at Wolverhampton Wanderers and he came close to fulfilling his dream of playing in the Premiership when Wolves lost to Bolton Wanderers in the 1994-95 play-offs. Despite having played against the Albion on six occasions (for Bradford, Sunderland and Wolves) he has only once scored against them – for Sunderland in 1994.

GOULD, BOBBY. Bobby Gould started off his career with the first of his 12 League clubs, his hometown Coventry City. He made his name with Arsenal, scoring their goal in their shock 3-1 defeat by Swindon Town in the 1969 League Cup final, but it was with Wolves that he had his greatest success, in two spells, 1970-71 and 1975-77. He was bought by Albion manager Don Howe to help keep Albion in Division One in September 1971, which he helped to do in his 60 games for the club (19 goals) before moving on to Bristol City, West Ham, Bristol Rovers, Hereford and Wimbledon. Never a popular player at The Hawthorns (with the fans or his colleagues) Gould invited antagonism because of his basic, direct style of play, but he had a fair scoring rate at all of his clubs. He became manager of Bristol Rovers in 1981 and did much to build up the Coventry FA Cup-winning side of 1987 during his 18-month spell at Highfield Road, later winning the FA Cup for himself with Wimbledon's 'Crazy Gang' in 1988. In 1991, he left his job as QPR coach to take over from Brian Talbot as manager at The Hawthorns, but was never welcomed by the Albion supporters because of his reputation as a devotee of the 'long ball game' and was dismissed after failing to win promotion from the Third Division at the end of his first full season. Within two weeks, Gould was installed as manager back at Highfield Road alongside Don Howe, but sensationally resigned from the Sky Blues after a defeat at Loftus Road in 1994. In September 1995 he was appointed manager of the Welsh international side.

GRAY, ANDY. Signed for Aston Villa from Dundee United for a

Bobby Gould

bargain £110,000, Andy Gray was a brilliant centre-forward in his heyday at Villa Park. He moved for a million pounds to Wolves in September 1979, where he won the League Cup final for them in a four-year stay at Molineux. In 1983, Howard Kendall took him to Goodison Park, where he helped to revitalise Everton's fortunes in a period when they won the League, FA Cup and the European Cup Winners Cup. He moved back to Villa Park in July

1985, and was actually playing as a centre-half in the Third Division on loan with Notts County when Ron Atkinson, a long-time admirer, swooped to sign him, initially on loan, for the Albion. Although his knees were by this time so bad that he was unable to train with the rest of the squad, Gray's goals (he was the Albion's top scorer in the 1987-88 season with ten goals) helped keep the club in the Second Division. Yet his main contribution, according to Atkinson, was in the dressing-room, where his knowledge and experience helped to motivate a struggling side. Gray made his Albion debut in a 3-3 draw at Plymouth, scoring twice, and played his last Albion game at Brighton exactly a year later, before moving to finish his playing career with his child-hood favourites Glasgow Rangers – where he finished with his first Scottish Championship medal, to add to his 20 full Scottish caps. He is now a presenter for BSkyB Sport.

GRIFFIN, FRANK. One of only three Albion players ever to have scored the winning goal in a Wembley final, Griffin was a clever, fast winger signed from Shrewsbury Town in April 1951, as a replacement for the badly injured Billy Elliott. A vital part of Vic Buckingham's attacking Albion side for eight years, including that 1954 FA Cup final against Preston, his big time career was effectively ended when he broke his leg in another FA Cup tie at home to Sheffield United in 1958. He did return to the side, but was never the same player, playing just three games before winding down his career with Northampton and Wellington Town.

GROUNDS, FORMER. From 1878 to 1880, the club utilised two pitches, at Cooper's Hill, off the Beeches Road, and in the newly opened Dartmouth Park, and the players carried their portable goalposts between the two pitches. By the start of the 1880-81 season, the club had a more or less permanent pitch in the Park, with changing facilities at the Glebe public house in nearby Reform Street. In August 1881, the club signed a nine-month lease for their first enclosed ground, the Birches, formerly Bunn's Field, in Walsall Street, near the centre of West Bromwich. Originally, the players had changing rooms at the White Hart public house, later moving to the Roebuck Inn. In September 1882, Albion were on the move again, to Four Acres, which they shared with local cricket club, the West Bromwich Dartmouth.

Naturally, they were restricted to only playing home games outside the cricket season, with matches only being allowed on Saturdays and Mondays throughout the season – although traditional half-day closing in West Bromwich was a Wednesday. With these restrictions in mind, the club only remained at the Four Acres for three seasons, moving the few hundred yards to a new site at Stoney Lane, which they took on a seven-year lease in February 1885, just before their greatest triumph to date, the FA Cup final. The new ground was to remain Albion's home for 15 years, a period which saw them rise to become a club of national renown, as founder members of the Football League and twice winners of the FA Cup. The first match to celebrate the opening of the new ground was a friendly fixture against the Third Lanark Rifle Volunteers, on 5 September 1885, a match won 4-1 by the Albion.

GROVES, WILLIAM. An early example of the 'play anywhere' utility player, Groves was bought by the Albion from Glasgow Celtic in October 1890, although, because of a suspension hanging over him from a brief spell as an Everton player (he never played for their first XI), he had to sit out his first month at the Albion. Whilst in West Bromwich, he was converted from his early position as an inside forward, to a steady wing-half, the position he played in the 1892 FA Cup final when the Albion beat Aston Villa 3-0. Such was the quality of Groves' performance in the Oval final that Villa swooped for the player in September 1893, paying £120 for the 24-year-old – the first player to rate a three-figure transfer fee. At the time, Albion were negotiating to transfer him back to Everton, when Villa approached him without the Albion's consent, an offence for which they were fined the huge amount, for those days, of £25. Groves went on to win a Championship medal with the Villa, before he finished his career with his two former clubs in Scotland, Celtic and Hibernian.

GUESTS. During World War Two, the more relaxed rules of the regionalised football leagues allowed clubs to play 'guest' players, often those stationed with the armed forces in that area. As a result, certain clubs, such as Portsmouth and Aldershot in particular, benefited very much from their proximity to military bases to be able to select teams full of former internationals. Albion used around 40 such guests, the most famous being Peter Doherty (Manchester City), Eddie Hapgood (Arsenal), Gil Merrick (Birmingham), Harry Parkes (Aston Villa), Peter McKennan (Partick), Jimmy Sanders (Charlton) and Jack Smith (Chelsea). The last three all returned to The Hawthorns after the war – Jack Smith as Albion's first full-time manager.

H

HAGAN, JIMMY. Jimmy Hagan was a marvellous scheming inside-forward at Bramall Lane, where he made over 400 appearances, and would have won far more than his solitary England cap had not World War Two intervened. Ironically, Hagan failed a trial as a youngster at The Hawthorns, only to return later as manager. Hagan finished his playing career with the Blades in 1958, and took over as manager at little Midland League club, Peterborough United. He took the Posh from non-League obscurity into the League and up through the divisions. In their first season in Division Four, they ran away with the title, scoring a League record of 134 goals. However, with Peterborough riding high in Division Three, Hagan was sacked in October 1962, after deep unrest had striven the club – the week before, seven senior players had demanded transfers. Hagan was out of a job for six months, despite his fine track record, until he was offered the job as Albion manager as successor to Archie Macaulay in April 1963. He had a great record at the Albion, being responsible for signing some excellent players who would go on to serve the club well in the years ahead, including John Kaye, Doug Fraser and Jeff Astle, and took the club to their first trophy success in over a decade when they won the Football League Cup in 1966, as well as finding some success in the First Division. Hagan's authoritarian nature, seen briefly at London Road, came to the surface again in

Ian Hamilton

December 1963, when Albion's England full-back, Don Howe, led a players' strike in protest against the new manager's 'lack of understanding'. Later in the month, a refusal by Hagan for the players to wear tracksuit bottoms during training in the bitterly cold winter led to a total of 20 players being involved in the dispute, which was only settled by the players backing down just before Christmas 1963. Howe was transferred to Arsenal the following April. Albion again reached the League Cup final in 1967, but they lost 3-2 at Wembley against Third Division Queens Park Rangers, after coasting two goals ahead at half-time; Hagan was dismissed shortly afterwards, in May 1967, once Albion's First Division future had been assured. Hagan went on to have successful spells as manager at Benfica (three Championships in as many years), Sporting Lisbon and Oporto.

HAMILTON, IAN. Ian Hamilton was signed by the Ardiles-Burkinshaw managerial pairing at the start of Albion's successful Second Division promotion campaign in 1992, providing much needed mobility in what had previously been an ageing midfield. By the end of the season, he was the only ever-present in the side, playing in 46 League games and three play-off matches as Albion beat Port Vale at Wembley to win promotion. Originally an apprentice with Southampton, Hamilton was surprisingly released from the Dell to go on to play for Cambridge United and Scunthorpe United, twice losing in the play-offs with the latter club before being successful at Wembley with the Albion. Hamilton has been a little less convincing in the First Division, where a tendency to dwell on the ball, and his low scoring record have counted against him, but despite often being the butt of the criticism of the Brummie Road end, he has kept his place almost continuously for the past four years.

HARTFORD, ASA. Another product of Albion's superb youth policy of the time, Richard 'Asa' Hartford was a skilful, energetic Scottish midfielder who first made his name with his goal-scoring exploits as an 18-year-old in Albion's first entry into the European Cup Winners Cup in 1968. By 1971 he had replaced fellow Scottish veteran Bobby Hope at the heart of the Albion's midfield 'engine-room' and was courted by Don Revie's Leeds United, signing for them that year for £170,000, only to see the move sensationally cancelled when it was discovered that he had a congenital heart defect. Hartford continued to shine for the Albion for another three years before leaving for Manchester City for £225,000. Subsequent moves to Everton, Nottingham Forest and a return to Maine Road saw him become one of the country's top midfielders, adding another 44 caps to the six Scottish caps he won whilst at The Hawthorns. Hartford went on to play for Norwich City, Bolton, Oldham and Stockport (as player-manager) and is now a coach with Blackburn Rovers.

HAT-TRICKS. For most seasons in their history, Albion have usually had at least one player scoring a hat-trick in League or Cup, but in recent years, with the lack of a true 'natural' goal-scorer, hat-tricks have been few and far between; before Hunt's treble in 1994, only 11 League hat-tricks had been scored by Albion players in the previous 23 years. W.G. Richardson leads the way in the hat-trick stakes, with 12 in the League. Cookson, who, like Richardson, played in the '30s when goals were a lot more commonplace, hit nine hat-tricks (including six goals in one game against Blackpool in 1927). In the '50s, Derek Kevan scored eight hat-tricks (including five goals against Everton in 1960) and Ronnie Allen hit seven. In the '60s and '70s, Jeff Astle and Tony Brown led the way, with six and five League hat-tricks respectively. Of the players currently still at the club, Andy Hunt has scored two hat-tricks, his first coming, remarkably, in his first full appearance for the club in April 1993. Lee Ashcroft and Kevin Donovan have scored one each (Donovan's coming in an 8-0 FA Cup win over non-League Aylesbury) but the club's most prolific goalscorer of recent times, 'SuperBob' Taylor, only recorded his first treble for the club as recently as March 1996, in the 4-4 draw with Watford at The Hawthorns, after 16 times registering two goals in a game.

HAWTHORNS, THE. By the turn of the last century, it was becoming obvious that a new ground was required for the club. They had been leasing Stoney Lane for 15 years, but because it was not owned by the club, they were reluctant to spend money on new stands and facilities, and it had gained a reputation as one of the poorer grounds in the Football League. It was certainly nothing to compare with the grandeur of, in particular, Villa Park, so the Albion board began to look around for a suitable piece of land. Surprisingly, they chose a field on the border with Smethwick and Handsworth, quite some distance away from the town centre of West Bromwich, but with the introduction of a new tram line to Birmingham it was felt that the site offered the best value for money possible, and a 14-year lease was signed in May 1900. The new ground was cleared and a grandstand erected in time for its official opening on 3 September 1900, a 1-1 draw with Derby County, but the club were relegated at the end of their first season at their new headquarters. The freehold of the ground was purchased for over £5,000, just before the end of the lease and, with the ground wholly owned by the club, a series of ground improvements were made to bring The Hawthorns, as the new stadium had been named, up to the standard of the other top grounds in the country. With the monies raised by the club's success just before and just after World War One, and the great promotion and FA Cup double in 1931, the ground was much improved with concrete terracing and wooden seats on the Handsworth and Halfords Lane sides of the ground, raising the capacity of the ground to around 70,000, a figure that was never actually tested, although a ground record 64,815 paid for entry to the FA Cup game with Arsenal in March 1937. In 1964, the 'Rainbow' Stand was erected at the Handsworth side of the ground, with the roof from that side being used to cover the popular Birmingham Road terracing for the first time. In 1979, the old Halfords Lane stand was replaced at a cost of £2 million and in 1994 the Birmingham Road and Smethwick End terraces were closed for the last time to enable the club to comply with the requirements of the Taylor Report. The new Smethwick End all-seater stand was opened for the home friendly with Kilmarnock on 3 September 1994. By Boxing Day, 1994, the Birmingham Road stand was completed and officially opened for the League game against Bristol City. The Hawthorns now has an official capacity of 25,800.

HEATH, NORMAN. Wolverhampton-born Heath joined the Albion during the war, playing in goal for Albion in the Wartime League in 1943, but not making his League debut until December 1947 – when he saved a penalty in a 2-1 win at Hillsborough. It took him until 1952 to end years of understudying first choice goalkeeper Jim Sanders, when he became a regular in Albion's finest side for over three decades. Tragically, Heath's football career ended with the 30-year-old on the brink of major honours, in a sickening collision with Sunderland's Ted Purdon at Roker Park in March 1954. At that time, Albion were top of the First Division and had just reached the FA Cup final, with Heath a major contributor to his club's success. Heath, paralysed with serious neck and back injuries, never played again, his Cup final place going to Jim Sanders. In April 1956, an amazing 55,497 people attended his testimonial match at The Hawthorns against an International XI.

HODGETTS, FRANK. Frank Hodgetts became the youngest ever player to take the field for the Albion when he played against Notts County in a wartime game in October 1940 – he was only 26 days past his 16th birthday. Frank went on to play for the Albion for another nine years, recording over 200 games for the club as, primarily, a left-winger. He left The Hawthorns for Millwall at the end of Albion's successful promotion campaign back to Division One in 1949, although, after being a regular for the previous seven seasons, he only played a very minor role in the promotion drive.

HOLLAND. Albion first went on tour to Holland before the start of the 1964-65 season. They played three games, losing 2-1 to Alkmaar before beating ADO (The Hague) 2-1 and top Dutch side, Ajax of Amsterdam, 1-0. The season before, Albion had beaten Alkmaar 2-1 at home in a mid-season friendly. Two years later, they were back in the Netherlands again, with Dutch side DOS Utrecht as the Albion's first opposition in a European competition – the Inter-Cities Fairs Cup. Albion drew 1-1 in Utrecht, and won 5-2 at The Hawthorns. In August 1982, Ron Wylie took an Albion side over to Holland again, and they beat Twente Enschede 3-1, and the following season, a full, three-match pre-season tour was arranged. Albion beat FC Den Bosch 3-0, Go Ahead Deventer 4-3 and drew 2-2 with NAC Breda. Coincidentally, one man to score in each of the three tour games on his home territory was Dutchman Maarten Jol.

HOPE, BOBBY. For most of the '60s, Albion's midfield was controlled by one man – Scotsman Bobby Hope. Legendary Liverpool manager Bill Shankly said of him, 'Stop Bobby Hope – and you stop Albion' during the epic sixth round FA Cup tie between Liverpool and Albion in 1968, and it was certainly true that if Hope had a bad game, then so did Albion. Hope made his Albion debut against Arsenal as a 16-year-old (the last amateur player to play for the club) in 1960 – within two years, he was a fixture in the side, creating many of the goals scored by the Kaye-Brown-Astle combination that scored so prolifically, particularly in Cup ties, in the mid-'60s. He made over 400 appearances for the club, winning FA Cup and League Cup winners' medals and scoring over 40 goals, the most memorable of which, perhaps,

Bobby Hope

came in the run to the final of the 1970 League Cup, when he chipped an 11-man wall on the Ipswich goal-line, from an indirect free-kick. In his early days at the club, Hope was often homesick for his native Scotland, and came close to signing for his boyhood heroes, Glasgow Rangers – had he indeed returned to Scotland, he would undoubtedly have won more than the two Scottish caps that he was awarded. Hope was sold by his former team-mate, Don Howe, in May 1972, finishing his playing career with Birmingham City and Sheffield Wednesday before taking over as manager of Bromsgrove Rovers, who he took to their highest ever placing near the top of the Vauxhall Conference, before resigning to concentrate on his business interests in 1994.

HOWE, DON. The home First Division match with Everton in August 1955 was an auspicious one – it marked the League debuts of two future England internationals. Most of the thunder was stolen by centre-forward Derek Kevan, who scored both goals, but at right-back, Don Howe had a very steady start to his career.

Don Howe

Within two years, he had won the first of what were to be 23 consecutive caps for England. He played nearly 400 games for the Albion, scoring 19 goals, mostly from the penalty spot, although he did have short spells in midfield and up front. Very outspoken as a player, he led the players' 'strike' at The Hawthorns in 1962-63, leaving the club the following year to sign for Arsenal, where a broken leg ended his playing career in March 1966. He became a coach at Highbury and was generally recognised as being the driving force behind the Arsenal side which won the League and Cup double in 1971, and he was appointed as Albion manager two months later, replacing Alan Ashman. Albion lost their reputation as a goalscoring, entertaining side when Howe sold all their age-ing stars (including Astle, Kaye and Hope) and introduced a more defensive-minded style of play but Albion were relegated to the Second Division for the first time in a quarter of a century. After two fairly unsuccessful years in the lower division, Howe resigned his post in April 1975. Subsequently, Howe coached with Galatasaray, Leeds, Arsenal (including a two year spell as manag-er), Wimbledon, Bristol Rovers, Coventry, QPR and England (under his former Albion colleague, Bobby Robson) and he is now a media commentator covering Italian football for Channel Four.

HUNT, ANDY. Andy Hunt was the final piece in the Ossie Ardiles promotion jigsaw in 1993. By April of that year, Albion's promo-tion drive was falling away, as they had no reliable goalscorer to support Bob Taylor apart from the ageing Simon Garner. Ardiles went back to his former club, Newcastle United, to sign reserve striker Hunt for £100,000. It was the bargain of the season, even though the player was obviously not fully match-fit; he only played five full games in the final run-in to the season, yet scored 11 goals, including a goal in his first appearance (as substitute for the last ten minutes) at Bradford, a hat-trick in his first full game at home to Brighton, and the vital opening goals in the play-off semi-final and final against Swansea and Port Vale, respectively. Although regarded as second fiddle to Bob Taylor, Hunt benefit-ed from Alan Buckley's passing style of play to become Albion's top scorer in 1994-95 and has matured to such a level that he will almost certainly be plying his trade in the Premiership in the near future, with Albion turning down million-pound bids for his ser-vices.

HUNDRED GOALS. Nine times in the club's history have Albion sides reached the magic figure of 100 goals during a season. The first team to do so were the 1893-94 side, who scored 106 goals in 47 League and Cup games. With defences getting tighter, it took another 27 years for an Albion team to reach the 'ton' again – but this time they did it exclusively in the League; the first team to do so, scoring 104 goals as Albion won the First Division for the only time in their history. After the changes in the offside law made goals easier to score, for a while, Albion hit 105 goals in the

Second Divison in 1929-30, then scored 103 in 1936-37 (League and Cup) by virtue of their run to the FA Cup semi-finals. Not surprisingly, the 100-goal mark was reached during Albion's attempt on the double in 1953-54 – 83 in the League and 20 FA Cup goals adding up to 103 in all. In 1958, they hit 112 League and Cup goals, a club record 119 in 1965-66, and, in European football for the first time, 110 in 1966-67. The last time that the ton was reached was in the Second Division promotion season of 1992-93, when Ossie Ardiles' attack-minded side scored 114 goals, in League, play-offs, FA Cup, Coca-Cola Cup and the Autoglass Trophy.

HUNT, STEVE. Albion's last player to be selected for England was Steve Hunt, who won two caps for his country in 1984. Rejected by his first club, Aston Villa, in 1977, he made a name for himself playing alongside Pele, Carlos Alberto and Franz Beckenbauer for New York Cosmos' all-conquering NASL side. He returned to English football with Coventry City, but was signed for Albion by Johnny Giles in March 1984, where he played some of the best football of his career, being capped for England after just a dozen appearances in the Albion midfield – a club record. Despite easily being Albion's best player in their disastrous relegation season in 1985-86, he was sold to Aston Villa, after a dispute over his best playing position, in March 1986, Albion receiving promising youngster Darren Bradley plus a cash adjustment. Within 18 months, Hunt had retired from football because of an arthritic knee and took up coaching positions with Willenhall, Port Vale and Aston Villa.

HURST, GEOFF. Geoff had long made his name when he arrived at The Hawthorns in August 1975, as the only man to score a hat-trick in a World Cup final, when England took the trophy in 1966. At his peak with West Ham and England, Hurst was a prolific goalscorer and target man. He played in over 500 games (and scored more than 200 goals) for West Ham, and was capped 49 times for England (24 goals). Unfortunately, when Albion manager Johnny Giles signed him for £20,000 from Stoke City, he was 33, and past his best. It was a bit of a panic buy, as Albion were struggling at the foot of Division Two, with a severe goalscoring problem, and Hurst just wasn't the answer. He played just a dozen games for the Baggies, scoring two headed goals, leaving for Seattle Sounders in the NASL on a free transfer in February 1976. Albion were his last League club as a player, for when he returned to England the following month, it was as player-manager of non-League Telford United, although he did later have a two-year spell as manager of Chelsea.

I

INTERNATIONAL MATCHES STAGED. Just two full England international matches have been staged at The Hawthorns, plus one Victory International. In October 1922, England beat Ireland 2-0, with Albion man Joe Smith as England right-back. Two years later, England beat Belgium 4-0 – in front of barely 15,000 spectators – and this time, Albion's Tommy Magee was in the England midfield. There have also been two public England trial matches played at the Hawthorns, England versus 'The Rest', in 1928 and 1935, whilst in February 1920, an England side beat 'The South' 2-1 on the ground.

IRELAND, REPUBLIC OF. Albion's first visit to what is now the Republic of Ireland was in May 1932, when they drew 0-0 with Shelbourne, in Dublin. They returned to Eire for an end of season tour in 1953 when they beat a Waterford Select XI (assisted by several English stars, including Stanley Matthews) 5-4 and a Bohemians Select XI, in Dublin, 5-1. Shortly after taking over as manager at The Hawthorns, the Republic's manager, Johnny Giles, took his side for a brief pre-season tour in July 1975; they beat Shamrock Rovers 1-0, but lost 1-0 to the now defunct side, Finn Harps. When Brian Talbot took his side to Ireland in successive seasons, 1989-90 and 1990-91, they met Shelbourne twice (4-2, 1-1), Cobh Ramblers (4-2) and Ards (4-0).

ITALY. Apart from the Anglo-Italian Tournament/Cup, which the Albion have entered on four occasions, Albion have three times played Italian club sides. In 1967, Albion lost at home and away to Bologna in the Fairs Cup competition. In 1970, whilst in Italy for the Anglo-Italian Tournament, Albion drew 1-1 in a friendly at Triestina, and they drew 2-2 in a friendly at AC Napoli in 1980 (*see* ANGLO-ITALIAN).

J

JOHNSTON, WILLIE. The Scottish winger was signed by Don Howe and although an immensely popular player with The Hawthorns regulars, Willie did not completely fulfil his obvious potential, although he is still fondly remembered as the best Albion winger of the past 30 years. Fast, skilful, with a fierce shot, Johnston's temperament was always against him – when he was signed, from Glasgow Rangers, he was actually serving a record ten-week suspension from Scottish football, and was sent off 15 times during his career, usually for fighting, and on one memorable occasion (at home to Brighton in the League Cup) for kicking the referee up the backside! Although Johnston was signed too late to prevent Albion's relegation in 1973, he was a vital part of Johnny Giles' promotion-winning side three years later, and went on to see Albion establish themselves as a top First Division side in 1978. He signed for Vancouver Whitecaps in March 1979, finishing his career back at Rangers, before moving as coach to Hearts and then Falkirk.

JOL, MAARTEN. Three years after Tottenham had started the trend for signing foreign stars, with Ardiles and Villa, Albion finally signed their first import when Ronnie Allen paid £250,000 to Dutch side Twente Enschede for Netherland international midfielder, Maarten Jol. Jol was Allen's first signing with the

Willie Johnston

money raised by the sale of Bryan Robson and Remi Moses to Manchester United, and at first the tall Dutchman looked a very useful purchase, with his tough tackling and excellent distribution. However, his tackling soon brought the disapproval of League referees and with it two sendings off (at Luton and at home to Tottenham in the League Cup semi-final) and a multitude of bookings. After numerous suspensions, Jol's form dipped dramatically and he was sold cheaply to Coventry City in October 1981. He played in only a handful of games at Highfield Road before returning to his native Holland, with his first professional club, FC Den Haag.

JONES, HARRY. Harry 'Popeye' Jones signed for the Albion as a centre-forward from Preston North End in May 1933, and was looked upon as an eventual replacement for W.G. Richardson. He was a bustling, aggressive type of forward, although not particularly strongly built, but he did have a goalscoring knack. He did not establish himself in the Albion first team until the 1936-37 season, despite some prodigious scoring for the Central League side, but once in the team, even managed to outscore his mentor, Richardson, to become the club's top scorer in the League that

107

season, with 17 goals to WG's 16. The following season – unfortunately the one when Albion were relegated to Division Two – Jones had taken over Richardson's centre-forward shirt, and was top scorer again in 1937-38 and 1938-39. Jones's best years were lost to the war. In the first season of wartime regional football, Jones scored 52 goals, including a club record run of a goal in 11 consecutive games, but hardly played for the club again, guesting during the war with Everton and Blackburn Rovers before retiring from the game with injury at the age of 31.

JORDAN, WILLIAM. *See* AMATEURS.

KAFFIRS. In November 1899, in their last season at Stoney Lane, Albion played hosts to a team known as African Kaffirs, who had already lost their other two tour games at Aston Villa (7-4) and Burton (9-8). Albion took it easy in the first half and were 6-4 down at the interval, before powering ahead to win 11-6.

KAYE, JOHN. Originally signed as a centre-forward from Scunthorpe United in May 1963 – and good enough to reach the final 40 for England's World Cup squad in 1966 – 'Yorky' Kaye was better known as a left-half, following his conversion by Albion manager Alan Ashman during the club's successful run in the 1968 FA Cup. A very hard player, Kaye played nearly 400 games for the Albion between 1963 and November 1971, when he was sold by his former Albion team-mate, Don Howe, to Second Division Hull City. After a spell as coach, Kaye took over as Hull's manager for two years, then followed that up with a four-year spell as assistant manager at Scunthorpe and then manager at his home town side, Goole Town, before retiring from football in 1983.

KENNEDY, JOE. Joe Kennedy was one of the best uncapped players ever to play for the Albion. A marvellous header of the ball, Joe started his playing career as an inside forward, coming in for the last eight games of the successful Second Division promotion campaign of 1949 – indeed, he scored his first goal for the club in the vital 3-0 win over Leicester City at Filbert Street in May 1949, which confirmed Albion's return to Division One that season. After several seasons in the side as a right half, Kennedy took over the centre-half position from the retiring Jack Vernon, the perfect foil to the more creative Ray Barlow, who really rated his team-mate. With the Wolves' Billy Wright to contend with in the England side, the best Kennedy could manage was three England 'B' caps as captain, but he also won an FA Cup winners' medal for the Albion in 1954, when he filled in at right-back for the injured Stan Rickaby, having earlier temporarily lost his place in the side to young Jimmy Dugdale. After 13 years at the Albion, Kennedy finished his League career at Chester, before moving into non-League as player-manager with Stourbridge, having made over 400 appearances for the Albion.

KEVAN, DEREK. Derek 'The Tank' Kevan was a centre-forward of the old school – tough, aggressive, with a great goal-scoring record. In 300 games for the Albion, he scored nearly 200 goals, including five goals in one First Division game against Everton in 1960. Although lacking a certain amount of finesse, Kevan made up for it with pure strength, often bulldozing his way through First Division and international defences – he scored eight goals in 14 England appearances, although his very selection ahead of more skilful players, such as Middlesbrough's Brian Clough, often courted controversy. Kevan was Vic Buckingham's first signing as Albion manager, when he bought him for £2,000 from his own former club, Bradford Park Avenue – good value for a player who was to remain at the Albion, usually as top scorer, for nearly ten years. In 1962, Kevan topped the First Division scoring charts with an Albion post-war best of 33 goals, and, the following year, when surprisingly sold to Chelsea after a falling-out with manager Archie Macaulay, he scored a hat-trick in his final Albion appearance. Another disagreement with Chelsea manager Tommy Docherty meant that he played just seven games for the Stamford Bridge side, later moving on to Manchester City, where his 30 goals helped the Maine Road side return to Division One. Unsuccessful spells at Crystal Palace, Peterborough and Luton Town followed, before he won the first medal of his career with

Fourth Division Champions Stockport County in 1967.

KEYS, MAJOR WILSON. Son of Harry, a leading figure in the Albion's history, Keys was elected to the Albion board in 1930, shortly after the death of his father, and he remained as a director until his retirement in 1965 – the longest-serving director in the club's history, beating William Bassett's tenure by three years. He became vice-chairman in 1937 and chairman in 1947, holding the position until his retirement in 1965. Four years after leaving the board, he was elected vice-president of the Football Association. He was a stern, authoritative figure throughout his time at the club, much feared by the players, and disliked by several managers because of his close control of transfer funds and what they felt was excessive interference in playing affairs at the club.

KEYS, HARRY. Harry Keys was first elected to the Albion board in 1899, but resigned after a dispute with his fellow directors three years later, returning, along with former player Billy Bassett to help save the club in its darkest hour, when it was perilously close to bankruptcy. He had two more, separate, spells as director, with a total of eight years as club chairman, totalling 14 years in all, until his death in 1929, when he was also vice-president of the Football League itself, the highest football office occupied by a West Bromwich director until Bert Millichip's election as head of the Football Association some 50 years later.

L

LEAGUE POINTS, HIGHEST, LOWEST. For many years, Albion's total of 60 points which they garnered whilst winning the League Championship in 1920 was the best the club has managed. Even after the League changed to the three points for a win system, poor results on the field for nearly a decade meant that the total would not be overtaken until 1989, when Brian Talbot's side that nearly reached the Second Division play-off managed to collect 72 points. The only other time the 60 point level has been beaten was when Ossie Ardiles took the team to promotion in 1993; the side reached fourth place in the new Division Two and collected a club record of 85 points. Albion's worst season for League points was in 1890-91 when they collected a mere 12 points from 22 games. Since the divisions have been expanded to ensure (at least) 42 games per season, Albion's worst performance has been the 24 points they achieved when they finished bottom of the First Division in 1985-86 – and that was with the three points for a win system (four wins and 12 draws).

LOAN PLAYERS. The system for loaning players has been in operation for quite a few years, but Albion rarely used it. Probably the first loan player to play for the Albion was Irish international Mick Martin, who was signed on temporary forms from Manchester United in October 1975, signing up properly in

December of that year to become a vital part of Johnny Giles' promotion midfield, and staying with the club for three great years. The situation changed after Albion fell into the Second Division in the mid-'80s, and consecutive Albion managers used the loan system to try out players 'on the cheap', often with an option to buy. In February 1988, Kenny Swain was signed by Ron Atkinson on two months' loan from Portsmouth – along with Andy Gray, who had earlier been signed on loan from Aston Villa before a permanent move was arranged, he made a crucial contribution to keeping Albion out of the Third Division that season. Bobby Gould signed Chelsea's Frank Sinclair and Bournemouth's Wayne Fereday on loan at the same time in December 1991. Fereday was signed permanently at the end of the loan period, but Sinclair was returned to Chelsea early after being sent off and suspended for head-butting the referee in a game at Exeter. During the following season Ossie Ardiles was trying to find a strike partner for Bob Taylor, and tried out former England international Luther Blissett, Alan Dickens, Scottish international David Speedie and Newcastle reserve Andy Hunt on loan, finally plumping for the latter after an inspired sequence of 13 goals in as many games in the final run-in to promotion from the Second Division.

LONGEST GAME. The longest competitive game in the Albion's history was the 1944 Midland War Cup final, second leg, played against Nottingham Forest at the City Ground. In the first leg, at The Hawthorns, the two sides drew 2-2. The two sides also drew 2-2 at the end of 90 minutes in the second leg, and each side scored a further goal in 20 minutes of extra time. In those days before the penalty shoot-out, that meant sudden death extra time, which Albion won with a goal from Ike Clarke in the 129th minute of play. The game had kicked off at 3 pm, and did not finish until 5.25 – 145 minutes, including the time it took the police to clear the pitch after an invasion by Forest fans who thought they had won the Cup two minutes from the end of the first period of extra time. The longest Albion Cup tie was in 1953, when Albion and Chelsea fought out four games in the fourth round of the FA Cup. They drew 0-0 at Stamford Bridge, then 1-1 at The Hawthorns, after extra time, moving on to Villa Park (1-1, after extra time) before Chelsea came out on top 4-0 at Highbury. In all, the tie lasted a total of 420 minutes.

M

MACAULAY, ARCHIE. Archie was a fine inside-right for Glasgow Rangers, West Ham and Arsenal, winning seven caps for Scotland, as well as representing Great Britain against the Rest of Europe alongside Albion's Jack Vernon in 1947. After a great start to his League management career at Carrow Road, where he took Norwich from the brink of re-election to fourth place in Division Two, and almost to an FA Cup final place whilst still a Third Division club in 1959, he was enticed away by the Albion to take over from Gordon Clark. He stayed at West Bromwich just 18 months, leaving in April 1963, to manage the 'other' Albion, at Brighton and Hove, and then drifted out of football in 1968. His spell at The Hawthorns was not a happy one; he was not particularly liked by the senior players at the club, and left complaining of directorial interference in playing affairs. His reign was encapsulated perfectly by a grainy, black and white documentary film made at the time for the Ford British Film Library, entitled *The Saturday Men*.

MAGEE, TOMMY. Tommy Magee is the only Albion player to win both FA Cup (1931) and Football League Championship (1920) medals with the club – and he added five England caps to those medals as well. Incidentally, Magee is still the smallest player ever to win a full cap for England. Signed whilst still in the trenches in

France in World War One, the diminutive Magee – he was ten stone and stood just five feet two inches – made his name as a combative right-half in nearly 500 games for the club between 1919 and 1934, when he signed for Crystal Palace as player-coach.

MANAGERS. Although Albion have had a phenomenal turnover of managers in the last 20 years (15 in that period), the club was once known as one of the most stable in the country. From 1902 to his retirement in 1948, the managerial as well as the secretarial duties were carried out by Fred Everiss, and it was he who must take the credit for the club's success in winning the League Championship in 1920 and the FA Cup and promotion in 1931. In 1948 it was decided to split the coaching and administrative roles and Jack Smith, who had guested for the Albion during the war, was appointed as Albion's first bona fide manager, taking the club back into Division One at the first attempt. He was dismissed in April 1952, and a 'chief coach', Jesse Carver, appointed, but he returned to coaching on the continent within eight months, to be replaced with the man who was to become one of Albion's greatest managers, Vic Buckingham. The former Spurs man made Albion into a great side during the '50s, winning the FA Cup in 1954 and going close to the Championship on more than one occasion. After Buckingham was sacked in 1959, the club went backwards for a while under Gordon Clark and Archie Macaulay, but found a strong attacking identity again under Jimmy Hagan, who took the club to two successive League Cup finals, as well as bringing in a nucleus of players (Kaye, Fraser, Astle) who were to serve the club well for many years. Hagan lost his job after the Queens Park Rangers debacle at Wembley in 1967, giving way to Alan Ashman, who won the FA Cup in his first season at the club. After four years in the job, when he failed to adequately replace a team of ageing players, Ashman was dismissed in favour of an Albion old boy, Don Howe, who had done such a good job coaching Arsenal to the League and Cup double the previous year. It was a disastrous move, as his regimented ideas on football alienated the older players and turned Albion from a free attacking side to a dour defensive outfit, losing their First Division place into the bargain. Howe was replaced in 1975 – and it was a rare, visionary move by the Albion board to bring in Johnny Giles as player-manager. He not only took the club back to the First Division at the first attempt, but laid the groundwork for a stunning revival of the club that was to last for over a decade. Giles resigned after two years because he felt he was being denied sufficient control of non-football matters at the club, and gave way to another former player, Ronnie Allen, who lasted just six months, without being offered a contract, before being lured overseas with a lucrative contract in Saudi Arabia. His replacement was Ron Atkinson, whose cavalier approach to the game made Albion the most attractive side in the country, before he was poached by Manchester United in 1981. That controversial move saw the return of Ronnie Allen in a season which had Albion reaching the semi-finals of both Cup competitions, but only securing First Division safety in the final home game of the season, a campaign which meant that Allen was 'kicked upstairs' in favour of Ron Wylie. Another backwards move, Wylie lasted for two and a half seasons of mediocrity before being replaced by the second coming of Johnny Giles. Unfortunately, Giles' second spell was nowhere near as successful as had been the first and after a dreadful start to the 1985-86 season, he resigned in favour of his brother-in-law, Nobby Stiles, who unwillingly acted as manager until Ron Saunders was appointed in February 1986. Albion continued to slide under Saunders, who was a mere shadow of the man who had guided Aston Villa to so much success, and, with the club at the bottom of the old Second Division, Ron Atkinson was persuaded to take the job for a second time. Atkinson saved the club from relegation, but left to manage Atletico Madrid, with team captain Brian Talbot taking the player-manager's job after a very successful trial period. Talbot went close to taking the side into Division One, but missed out on the play-offs and then lost his way tactically as well, and was dismissed after the horrific home defeat by Woking in January 1991. After a damaging two-month delay, Bobby Gould was appointed manager, but not soon enough to prevent relegation to Division Three, and when he failed to effect an immediate return to the Second Division, he was dismissed as well. Former World Cup star Ossie Ardiles had one, glorious season at the helm, in which his team played some magnificent attacking football to squeeze past Port Vale in the play-off final at Wembley, but once more Albion fans felt betrayed when he, also without a contract, left for Tottenham in the summer of 1993. Ardiles was replaced by his former assistant, Keith Burkinshaw, who was much more defensively minded, and the team flirted with relegation for two seasons before he was replaced by the current manager, Alan Buckley, in October 1994.

MANAGERS, INTERNATIONAL. Albion have had four players who have managed international sides. In October 1956, former wing-half Jimmy Murphy took on the role of part-time manager of Wales, in addition to his full-time job as assistant manager of Manchester United, taking Wales to what is, so far, their only appearance in the finals of a World Cup tournament, in 1958. Nearly 40 years later, Bobby Gould, a former Albion player and manager, was appointed as full-time manager of Wales, too late to prevent their elimination from the 1996 European Championship finals. When Johnny Giles arrived as Albion's player-manager in June 1975, he had been part-time player-manager of the Republic of Ireland for two years, a position he retained until April 1980. The ultimate managerial appointment for an English-born Albion player, though, is manager of the England side, and in July 1982, former Albion inside-right Bobby Robson achieved that position, after 13 years as manager of Ipswich Town. In 1990, he stepped down after taking England to the brink of the World Cup final in Italy, when his side lost in the semi-finals on penalties to West Germany. Robson's number two in the England set-up for many years was his former Albion colleague, Don Howe, whilst Terry Venables' assistant for England has been another former Albion star, and an England manager of the future, Bryan Robson.

MARDON, PAUL. Bristol-born Mardon is Albion's only current international, being selected by Welsh manager Bobby Gould for the European Championship game against Germany in October. A fast, strong, elegant central defender or full-back, Mardon started his career under manager Terry Cooper at Bristol City, moving with his boss to Birmingham City, where he attracted the attentions of Graeme Souness' Liverpool, missing out on a possible move there by badly injuring his ankle whilst on trial at Anfield. Mardon was signed by Keith Burkinshaw in November 1993, and slotted straight into a fragile Albion defence, but he carried with him a reputation from St Andrews that he was a defender prone to making expensive mistakes, which has taken him a couple of years to live down. He has also had a fair number

Paul Mardon

of injuries during his career, but on form is clearly one of the coolest defenders in the Endsleigh League, and quite capable of excelling at a higher level.

MARKSMEN, LEAGUE. Just six times have Albion players topped the scoring charts for their division. In 1920, Freddie Morris was the First Division's top scorer with 37 goals. Eight years later, Jimmy Cookson's 38 goals was the best in the Second Division that season, whilst Ronnie Allen (27 goals in 1955), Derek Kevan (33 goals in 1962), Jeff Astle (25 goals in 1970) and Tony Brown (28 goals in 1971) all came out on top at the end of the season, Kevan sharing top spot with a future Albion player, Ray Crawford.

MARKSMEN, MOST FEARED. Certain strikers seemed to have a bit of a soft spot for the Albion over the years, and invariably seemed to score against them almost every time they played them. In the early days of the League, John Southworth of Everton was never a popular player amongst Albion supporters, not surprisingly, because as well as a number of other goals in other meetings, he scored a record-breaking six goals against the Albion in a 7-1 defeat at Anfield in December 1893 (and that just three days after Albion had won 8-0 at Molineux!). Five players have scored five goals in a game against the Albion, with pride of place going to Freddie Steele, who scored his in Albion's club record defeat, when they lost 10-3 at Stoke City in February 1937. Steele, whose son played one League game for Albion in the '50s, was a regular thorn in Albion's flesh, and scored a host of goals against the Baggies; six years after that record haul, he scored another four goals in a Wartime League Cup game at The Hawthorns – which Stoke won by 8-2, Albion's worst-ever defeat at The Hawthorns in a competitive game. In modern times, with better defences and less open, attacking football, goals in general have become harder to get, but three players have stood out as prolific goalscorers against the Albion. The most outstanding, of course, was Jimmy Greaves, another player who scored five against the Albion, for Chelsea, in a 7-1 win at Stamford Bridge in December 1960. Albion supporters were sorry when he returned so quickly from his spell in Italy, because he continued to knock in the goals for Tottenham and also even in his brief spell at West Ham, where he scored a winner deep in injury time to push Albion closer to relegation in 1973. In all, for his three clubs, Greaves hit 15 goals against the Albion, 1957-73. In the '70s, Albion's chief scourge was Newcastle's and Arsenal's Malcolm MacDonald, who scored 12 goals in only nine games, including a hat-trick at Highbury in a 4-0 Arsenal win in 1978. More recently, the player who has caused Albion defenders the most problems is Tottenham's Teddy Sheringham, although, amazingly, he did all the damage whilst playing for Millwall. His total, which included two hat-tricks, was ten in seven games.

MILLARD. LEN. 'Dependable' Len Millard signed for the Albion as a centre-forward in 1937, scoring a number of goals for the club in wartime football, but later switched to become a sturdy left-back, stopping at the club for an amazing 21 years, recording a then club record 650 appearances, many as captain. Very few wingers, including the greats such as Stanley Matthews and Tom Finney (who Len had 'in his pocket' in the 1954 FA Cup final), got the better of Millard, who rarely missed a game during his peak, and who was still playing for the Albion at the age of 39.

MILLICHIP, SIR 'BERT'. Bert Millichip became an Albion director in 1964, taking over as club chairman from Jim Gaunt in September 1974, a position which he held until his resignation in August 1984. Three years earlier, he had been elected chairman of the Football Association, the most senior position ever held by an Albion director, from which he retired after the European Championships in 1996. Millichip's ten years as chairman were amongst some of the most exciting times in the club's history, as the club went from the Second Division to a position challenging Liverpool for the First Division title, as well as being England's representatives in the first visit of a Western professional club to China, in 1978, a tour on which Millichip was a prime mover.

MILLS, DAVID. Mills was the one serious mistake in the transfer market that manager Ron Atkinson will readily admit to. Yet at the time, the transfer did not seem to be that much of a gamble, apart from the rather inflated price-tag. Atkinson had just had a bid of £750,000 for Trevor Francis turned down from Birmingham City, so instead, he turned to Middlesbrough's David Mills, who had an excellent goal-scoring record of nearly 100 goals in 350 games for his only League club. He had also won eight Under-23 caps with England, and was called into the full England squad during Joe Mercer's brief spell as England manager, although he never actually played a game. Atkinson saw the player as a ready-made replacement for the ageing Tony Brown, and paid over half a million pounds for him in January 1979 – Britain's costliest player until Trevor Francis moved to Nottingham Forest for £1 million shortly afterwards. Mills' problem was that he could not get into Albion's great team of that period, and that he had signed too late to play in Albion's UEFA Cup matches, so he spent most of that season on the substitutes bench. When he did make his full debut, at Highfield Road in March 1979, he had what was to be his best game in an Albion shirt, scor-

David Mills

ing one and making another in a 3-1 win. By the end of the season, he had actually replaced a stale-looking Laurie Cunningham in the Albion side, but never looked convincing. The following season, when Cunningham and Cantello had left, there were places up for grabs, but an Achilles tendon injury sustained in a testimonial at Birmingham at the end of the previous season meant that Mills was not fit enough for contention. Mills flitted in and out of the side over the next four years, but rarely looked the part, and after just 55 full games (nearly £10,000 per appearance!) Albion took a half a million pound loss on the deal by selling him to Sheffield Wednesday, in January 1983. That move was also not a success, but he fared better at Newcastle, where he played alongside John Trewick and Kevin Keegan in the 1983-84 season. He was released from St James Park at the end of that season, moving down through the ranks via Middlesbrough and Darlington, before ending up as player-coach at lowly non-

League Whitby Town in 1987. It was there that Mills suffered terrible injuries in a car crash which also killed his father, and he was forced to retire from football after a long period in hospital, moving into the local media. Ron Atkinson took an Albion side to Whitby for Mills' testimonial game in March 1988, Albion winning 8-0 in a match reduced to 80 minutes because of the terrible weather, a fact which accounted for the attendance of just 290 people, which raised less than £1,000 for the player.

MORLEY, TONY. Tony Morley is one of four holders of a European Cup winners medal to play for the Albion, won during their days at rivals Aston Villa (along with Kenny Swain, Ken McNaught, Nigel Spink and, in various friendlies, one-time Albion assistant manager, Dennis Mortimer). Starting off as an apprentice with Preston, Morley moved to Burnley, from where he was signed by the Villa, and he was a key figure in the brilliantly successful team in the early '80s, helping them win the First Division title in 1981 and setting up the winning goal for Peter Withe in the European Cup final a year later. Those performances for the Villa won him six full England caps. The speedy left winger was a surprise signing from the Villa by Ron Wylie in December 1983, but he only played 33 games for the Albion before leaving, initially for loan periods, with Birmingham City and then Seiko of Hong Kong, for FC Den Haag in Holland, who paid £25,000 for the player in 1986. A year later, he rejoined the Albion, on a two-year contract, and went on to make another 30 appearances under Ron Saunders (again) and Ron Atkinson. His final game for the Albion was the vital 3-1 win at Huddersfield which helped to maintain Albion's Second Division place in 1988.

MORRIS, FRED. Tipton-born Freddie Morris was a quality goalscoring inside-left who made a significant contribution to Albion's solitary Championship winning side of 1919-20, his 37 League goals that season setting a new club scoring record. Signed from Redditch, he had a 13-year career at the Albion, interrupted by World War One, but three times he was the club's top scorer in a season, and was also the first Albion player to reach the tally of 100 League goals whilst playing for the club. Morris was twice capped for England in 1920, and in 1919 became the first Albion player to score five goals in a League game.

MURPHY, JIMMY. Although playing over 200 games for the Albion, including the 1935 FA Cup final, Jimmy 'Spud' Murphy is now far more famous for his association with Manchester United. Albion signed him from local football in Wales in 1928 and groomed him to replace the ageing Tommy Magee at right-half, which he did admirably from 1931 to 1938, winning 15 caps for the full Welsh side, eventually leaving the club for Swindon Town at the end of the last pre-war season. Whilst serving overseas during the war, Murphy became associated with Matt Busby, and joined him as his assistant at Manchester United after the war (although not receiving the official title of assistant manager until 1955). Murphy was also part-time manager of the Welsh national side from 1956 to 1963, taking them to the World Cup quarter-finals in Sweden in 1958 – their only appearance, so far, in the final stages of the World Cup. After the Munich Disaster of 1958, when Busby was critically injured, Murphy took over the running of the side until Busby could return, and stopped at Old Trafford through all the club's glory days of the '60s, culminating in their great European Cup win in 1968.

N

NAYLOR, STUART. Ron Saunders' first signing after his appointment as Albion manager in February 1986 was Lincoln goalkeeper Stuart Naylor, who cost £110,000, the most Albion have ever paid for a goalkeeper. A former England Youth international, Stuart won three England 'B' caps whilst at The Hawthorns, and performed steadily between the posts in his ten years at the club, occasionally losing his place, for brief spells, to Mel Rees, Andy Dibble and Paul Bradshaw. An indifferent spell of form in 1993 saw him replaced by Tony Lange, who was the man in possession for the crucial run-in to promotion, including the glamour of a Wembley final against Port Vale, but he made the Albion number one shirt his own again, for his testimonial season, 1995-96, and became the first Albion goalkeeper to pass the 400 League appearance mark, until the signing of former England international keeper Nigel Spink from Aston Villa in February. He had a testimonial game against Coventry City at The Hawthorns in May 1995 and was granted a free transfer at the end of the season.

NEWSPAPER. The first attempt at an Albion club newspaper was made in 1979, when the Stockport Messenger Group published a 24-page tabloid, the *Throstle News*, as one of a number of publications for First Division clubs at that time. With Albion struggling in the League, it folded after just one issue. In February 1993, *The*

Stuart Naylor

Baggies was launched as the official club newspaper under the editorship of Glenn Willmore, and by the end of the 1995-96 season had published 37 issues. A popular, independent-minded 24-page colour tabloid newspaper, *The Baggies* covers all Albion first and second team games, as well as featuring interviews with current and former players, glossy colour posters and articles of general and historic interest to all Albion fans. More details, sample issues

(£1.50 inc. postage) and subscriptions (£17.00 per annum, inc. postage) can be obtained from: *The Baggies*, 54 Newhall Street, West Bromwich, West Midlands B70 7AQ.

NICHOLLS, JOHN. Along with his striking partner, Ronnie Allen, Johnny Nicholls ('Johnny on the Spot') is one of the best-known and best-loved of Albion's stars from the '50s – yet his Albion first team career was a remarkably brief one. After an early association with his home town club, Wolverhampton Wanderers, he was signed to the Albion by manager Jack Smith in 1950. He was thrown into the deep end for his Albion debut, as a late replacement for Ronnie Allen in the big FA Cup fifth round match at Ewood Park in February 1952, against Second Division Blackburn Rovers, after the centre-forward had injured his eye during training. John had a fair debut, as Albion lost 1-0, then went on to score five goals in a dozen League appearances that season. The following season, under new coach Jesse Carver, Albion were challenging for the Championship, finally ending up in fourth place in the First Division, and Nicholls just flitted in and out of the side, again scoring a meagre five goals, this time in 23 games, so it was some surprise when he started the 1953-54 season in such lethal form. Nicholls was Albion's top League scorer that season, with 28 goals, and formed a deadly partnership ('The Terrible Twins', as they were nicknamed at the time) with Ronnie Allen. Between them, in League and Cup, the two strikers scored 66 goals, propelling Albion to second place in Division One, and winning them the FA Cup at Wembley. That was quite a season for Nicholls, for he won the first of two England caps against Scotland on his birthday at Hampden Park in April 1954, playing alongside Ronnie Allen, and scoring in a 4-2 win. Unfortunately, that was also the same day that Albion met Wolves at The Hawthorns in what was to be the Championship decider – stripped of its two goalscorers, the Albion side lost 1-0, and went on to lose the title itself. The decline in Nicholls' career had already begun by the following season, put down by Nicholls himself as due to a bad ankle injury he sustained whilst jumping a gate in his brother's garden. He only managed another 20 League goals in 60 games in the following three seasons, moving for £4,000 for a brief, but very unhappy spell at Cardiff City (May-November 1957, two goals in eight games) before enjoying a successful two years at lowly Exeter City, where he found his scoring boots once more, with 23 goals in 55 appearances in the Third Division South. After drifting through the non-League scene with Worcester and Wellington Town, John retired from pro football in 1961. He died of a heart attack, whilst returning from an Albion game against Middlesbrough, in April 1995.

NICKNAMES. West Bromwich Albion have a number of nicknames. In the town itself, 'Albion' is the usual abbreviation, and it is a sure sign of a 'non-local' supporter if he uses the common epithet, 'West Brom'. For many years, the club was known as 'The Throstles'; apart from certain club programmes, this is now dying out, although a throstle, or thrush, is still prominent on the club's official badge. The name came from a period in the club's early history when the then secretary, Tom Smith, needed a symbol for the club crest, and chose the common thrush because of its widespread occurrence around the Black Country. In the '30s, the club kept a live throstle in a cage above the players' tunnel at every home game at The Hawthorns. The term has certainly been a godsend for journalists and cartoonists over the years, as a convenient way to represent the Albion's battles with 'The Wolves', 'The Heathens' and 'The Villains' in local derby games. Most popular with local supporters nowadays is 'The Baggies', a term whose derivation seems lost in the mists of time. One-time Albion secretary Eph Smith gave the explanation that the term was a reference to the baggy shorts worn by Amos Adams at the turn of the century, and a similar story is told about long-serving goalkeeper Joe Reader, who was one of the last custodians to discard the old, long baggy trousers in favour of knee-length shorts. Another story tells that the name is a corruption of the surname of Albion captain Tommy Magee, but in fact, 'The Baggies' was current long before Magee joined the club during World War One. More plausible is a story connected with the club's troublesome financial difficulties in the early years of the century. Such were the dire straits that the club was in, that supporters used to tour local pubs collecting money, for the 'Albion Shilling Fund'. These collections were made in little bags, and the followers, and hence the club itself, became known as 'Baggies'. The term, once definitely not in favour with the club itself, is now becoming popular all over the country, and is the name of what was the club's official newspaper, *The Baggies*, which was launched in 1993.

NON-LEAGUE CLUBS. Obviously, Albion met many non-League clubs in the FA Cup in the early days of the Football League, and occasionally lost to them, with defeats by Tottenham (in the 1901 semi-final), Southampton and West Ham being particularly notable. It was only after the formation of the two sections of the Third Division in the early '20s that defeats by non-League sides in the Cup could be considered to be particularly unusual, and in the 70 years, 1921-91, Albion were only drawn against non-League opposition in two occasions. In 1924, they beat the famed amateur side, Corinthians, by five clear goals at The Hawthorns in the second round, and in 1937, on the way to the semi-final, they beat little Spennymoor United 7-1 at home, in the third round. On 5 January 1991 came what was probably the lowest point in the club's history, when they were humiliated 4-2 at home by Diadora League side Woking, with Tim Buzagalo's hat-trick making Albion a laughing stock around the country as the club went on to drop into Division Three for the first time. Having to compete in the first round proper of the FA Cup meant that Albion's chances of drawing a non-League side had increased significantly – and they met four in the following three seasons. In 1991-2, they beat Marlow 6-0 at home, and a year later, also in the first round, they beat Aylesbury 8-0, with Kevin Donovan scoring Albion's first FA Cup hat-trick for 20 years. That win gave the Baggies a difficult away tie with Vauxhall Conference leaders Wycombe Wanderers, who were beaten only after a replay. In 1993-94, the club was stunned again, when they travelled up to the Shay for a first round tie, only to be beaten 2-1 by struggling Conference side Halifax.

NORTHERN IRELAND. Albion's first trip to Northern Ireland came in April 1893, when they played two games in Belfast, losing both, 3-1 to Linfield Athletic and 1-0 to an Ulster Select XI. Ten years later, they again played in Belfast, where they drew 5-5 with the Distillery club. It was not until 1932 that the Albion played in Belfast again, as part of a two-match tour; this time they beat Linfield 5-1. It was Linfield again who were the opponents in 1981, when Albion won 2-0. Albion went on pre-season tours to Northern Ireland (and the Republic) in successive seasons,

1989-90 and 1990-91. They met Glentoran twice (3-2, 0-0) and Newry Town (3-1).

O

OLDEST PLAYER. The oldest man to play for the Albion in a Football League game is the great Jesse Pennington, who played his last game for the club at the age of 38 years and 256 days, in the final match of the 1921-22 season, at Liverpool. Immediately afterwards, Pennington was examined by the Albion doctor and advised to retire from the game, because of an enlarged heart. The oldest player to sign for the Albion was Nigel Spink, who made his first appearance for the club at Ipswich in February 1996 – at the age of 37 and 179 days. If Spink sees out the whole of his two-and-a-half-year contract, he will pass Pennington's record some time near the end of the 1997-98 season.

ONES THAT GOT AWAY. Every top club has made mistakes by releasing players who have gone on to greater things with other sides. Mercifully, this happened relatively rarely with the Albion, at least in the past, but the number of players Albion have rejected but who have come back to 'haunt' the club has increased dramatically in recent years. Steve Bull is the name that most supporters will recall, as he went on to score hundreds of goals for local rivals Wolves and to play for England – Andy Thompson, sold to Wolves along with Bull, has also made out a good career for himself at Molineux. Amongst the players who could well have signed for the Albion, but were rejected after trials, were Jimmy

Hagan (Sheffield United, later Albion manager), Lee Sharpe (Manchester United) and Andre Kanchelskis (Everton).

OSBORNE, JOHN. In 1977, John Osborne became the first Albion goalkeeper ever to qualify for a long service testimonial. He was signed from Chesterfield in 1967, missing out on a Wembley League Cup final place against QPR because he was Cup-tied. He more than made up for that disappointment the following year when he was a key member of the side that won the FA Cup at Wembley against Everton, and he made another appearance at the Empire Stadium in 1970 – ironically because new goalkeeper Jim Cumbes was Cup-tied – when Albion lost 2-1 to Manchester City in the League Cup final. Around the time of that Wembley win, Ossie made quite a reputation as a 'Quiz-King' on BBC TV's football-based general knowledge game *Quizball*, which an Albion side won in 1968. Amazingly, Ossie retired from the game in 1972 – disillusioned with the Don Howe regime at the time – but returned six months later and, after three games on loan at Fellows Park, went on to play for the Albion for a further five years, setting a new club record of 22 clean sheets during the club's Second Division promotion campaign of 1975-76, and finishing with a total of over 312 games in an Albion jersey. By the start of the 1977-78 season, he had lost his place to up-and-coming young keeper Tony Godden, and he left the Albion after his testimonial game in 1978 to rejoin Johnny Giles at Shamrock Rovers, breaking his retirement on two occasions later to sign as an emergency non-contract player with Coventry and Preston. Until recently, Osborne was the commercial manager at Worcestershire CCC.

OVERSEAS PLAYERS. The first foreign-born player to play for the Albion first team was Gibraltar-born Alexis Suave, who played one Birmingham Cup game for the club in 1890 – and scored a hat-trick! It was to be another 80 years before another 'foreigner' wore the blue and white stripes, when Vancouver-born Glen Johnson made the first of four appearances in the First Division side in 1970. In 1977, Cyrille Regis, born in Maripiasoula, in French Guyana, made his Albion debut, scoring twice in a home League Cup tie with Rotherham, and later that same season, Grenada-born Brendan Batson was signed from Cambridge

United and played his first game at Birmingham City. After the first successful foreign 'imports' were introduced by Tottenham in 1978, overseas-born players became a lot more common in the Football League, and Albion soon had three such players on trial. In 1978, Rhodesian Bruce Grobbelaar played in goal for the Albion in a testimonial game at Motherwell, but Albion could not get the player a work permit, and he was allowed to leave for Vancouver. A year later, Albion were looking at another goal-keeper, Yugoslavian Ivan Katalinic, and played him in their cente-nary game against Ajax. He gave an impressive performance, and kept a clean sheet in a 1-0 win, but Albion decided not to take up the option, and he ended up at Southampton, where he made 48 League appearances. The following season, Albion brought over another Yugoslavian international, midfielder Dragan Muzinic, a friend of Katalinic's, and he played – and scored – in a pre-season friendly at Swindon, in August 1980, but Albion once again decid-ed against signing the player, who went on to play 20 games for Norwich City. Albion finally signed a player from an overseas side in 1981. Manager Ronnie Allen had already tried to sign a couple of players from his former club, Athletico Bilbao, but without suc-cess, so, with the recommendation of his former Albion colleague, Bobby Robson, he turned to Holland, and signed tough-tackling midfielder, Maarten Jol, for £250,000 from Twente Enschede. The tall Dutch international midfielder was signed as a replace-ment for Bryan Robson, a difficult enough task by itself, but after a solid start, the player's disciplinary record began to take its toll (he was sent off twice for the Albion in just over two years at the club, including the high profile League Cup semi-final against Tottenham in 1982) and his form dropped and he was sold cheap-ly to Coventry at the end of the 1983-84 season. Later in the 1981-82 season, Allen again went to Holland – and came back with another Dutch international, Romeo Zondervan, born in Surinam, who cost £225,000 from the same club as Jol. Zondervan, a mobile midfielder, left about the same time as Jol, both players playing their last game at Notts County in March 1984, shortly after Johnny Giles returned to the club. Zondervan moved on to a far more successful career at Ipswich Town, where he was often to torment the Albion in later years. In 1990, Icelandic international, Vetle Andersen made one substitute appearance for the Albion against Bournemouth, and two years later, ironically, under Albion's first foreign-born manager, Ossie Ardiles, Jamaican-born, but English international Luther Blissett played three games on loan from Watford. The latest 'foreigner' to play for the Albion first team is Amsterdam-born Richard Sneekes, who made his first team debut after signing from Bolton in March 1996. The club had a whole host of players on trial in the reserve side, including Zambian international goalkeeper Dave Chabala (who later died, with all of his Zambian international team-mates in a horrific plane crash) and Polish international full-back Janusz Gora.

P

PALMER, CARLTON. Tipton-born Palmer came up through the Albion ranks as a gangly, awkward full-back who was given his First Division debut by manager Nobby Stiles in 1985. He finally made a position in the first team his own as a hard-working midfielder under Ron Atkinson at the start of the 1988-89 season and his sale by Brian Talbot to Sheffield Wednesday in February 1989 (when Ron Atkinson had taken over as manager) possibly cost Albion promotion at the end of that season. Since then, Palmer has fully established himself as a Premiership player, winning 14 full England caps under Graham Taylor, and moving to Leeds United for £2.5 million.

PEARSON, HAROLD. Harold signed for the Albion in April 1925, so that for a year, both Pearsons, father and son, were on the club's books. With his 12-year stay at The Hawthorns, it meant that there had been a Pearson in goal at the club for an uninterrupted period of 31 years when Harold finally moved to Millwall at the start of the 1937-38 season, after over 300 games in the Albion goal, including two appearances in Wembley FA Cup finals (1931 and 1935). Although perhaps not quite the equal of his father as a keeper, he achieved the ambition that Pearson père missed out on – a full England cap, awarded against Scotland at Wembley in 1932.

Carlton Palmer (right)

PEARSON, HUBERT. The first of a unique two generation goal-keeping family at The Hawthorns. Hubert joined the club in February 1906, winning First and Second Division Championship medals in 1920 and 1911, as well as appearing in the 1912 FA Cup final, missing out on an England cap through injury after being selected to play in 1923. Hubert, father of Harold, is unique amongst Albion goalkeepers in that he is the only player in that position to score a goal for the club in a League game – he scored two penalties in the 1911-12 season!

PEARSON, TOM. Albion's first quality goalscorer in the Football League – in fact, he was Albion's top goalscorer in the competition in their first five seasons. A superb inside forward whose partnerships with several more burly centre-forwards, including Bayliss and Groves, helped Albion reach three FA Cup finals, in 1888, 1892 and 1895. After playing over 200 games for the club, and scoring over 100 goals, Pearson was forced to retire from the game after suffering serious injury in 1894.

PENALTY SHOOT-OUTS. Albion have only ever been involved in four penalty shoot-outs at first team level – and they've lost three of them! The first came in the 1971 Watney Cup final, when they lost 4-3 on penalties after a 4-4 draw against Colchester United at The Hawthorns. Tony Brown, Jeff Astle and Bobby Hope, who had all scored from the spot in League games, all scored – Len Cantello and Ray Wilson, neither regular penalty takers, missed. In 1978, Albion were defending their title as holders of the Tennant-Caledonian Cup (*see* PRE-SEASON TOURNAMENTS) but could only draw 1-1 with Southampton in the semi-final at Ibrox Park. The penalty shoot-out was another disaster, with Albion losing 3-1, with Tony Brown the only Baggie on target. Next, in the relegation of 1985-86, Albion drew 2-2 at home to Chelsea in the Southern Area semi-final of the new Full Members Cup (after losing a two-goal lead). After extra time, Albion lost 5-4 on penalties – Steve Bull, Steve Hunt, Imre Varadi and Andy Thompson scored; ironically, Albion's man of the match, and goalscorer, Garth Crooks, hit the post with his spot kick. The Baggies finally broke their duck in January 1996, in the English semi-final of the Anglo-Italian Cup against Birmingham City at St Andrews. After equalising through Paul Raven 11 minutes from time, to force a 2-2 draw (which was how it remained after 30 minutes extra time) Albion won a place in the English final against Port Vale by scoring all of their four penalties, to the home side's one. Andy Hunt, Bob Taylor and Lee Ashcroft (all three current club penalty takers) scored the first three, to put Albion 3-0 ahead, and former Blues man David Smith scored the winning spot-kick.

PENNINGTON, JESSE. 'Peerless' Pennington was the finest fullback of his generation. After a spell as an amateur with Aston

Villa, Jesse signed for the Albion in 1903 and remained with the club until his enforced retirement, on medical grounds, some 19 years later. He played over 500 times for the Baggies, a record that stood for over 50 years until broken by Tony Brown, winning 25 England caps, several as captain. He captained Albion to their only First Division Championship in 1920 and the Second Division Championship in 1911, as well as winning an FA Cup runners-up medal in 1912.

PERRY, CHARLIE. One of three Perry brothers to play for the Albion at the end of the last century, Charlie was a cool, dynamic centre-half who was capped three times for England, and played in four FA Cup finals for the Albion (1886, 1887, 1888, 1892). He played in every round of the FA Cup run to the final in 1895, but missed out on the final itself after seriously injuring his knee in a Birmingham Cup semi-final against Small Heath. Ironically, a similar injury to previous centre-half Fred Bunn, also on the eve of the Cup final, in 1886, had given Perry his big break, when the directors decided to play the young reserve in the final after just a handful of first team games. The injury was so severe that it ended Perry's career the following season, after over 300 games for the club; he was later a director for six years, from 1896 to 1902.

PERRY, TOM. Tom Perry, brother of Charlie and Walter, joined the Albion from Stourbridge in 1890, and played for the club for 11 years, often at right-half alongside Charlie, in well over 300 games for the club, including the 1895 FA Cup final. A 'utility' player, who could play in defence, midfield and as a winger, Tom was a key player for the club until his sale to rivals Aston Villa in 1901 – he won one England cap, in 1898.

PERRY, WALTER. The third of the Perry brothers, he had two spells with the club, as a forward, 1886 to 1889 and 1894 to 1895, but only played around 50 games all told, never reaching the heights of his two brothers, Tom and Charlie.

PLAY-OFFS. The modern version of the play-offs were introduced for the 1986-87 season, and in that year, and the following one, Albion only just escaped having to play the top teams in Division Three to avoid relegation by a margin of three and two points, respectively. By 1988-89, the team had improved enough under Brian Talbot to be chasing the play-offs at the other end of the table, but a club record haul of 72 points was still four points too short to qualify. In 1993, under Ossie Ardiles, Albion finished fourth in the (new) Second Division, and qualified for a two-legged semi-final with Swansea City. They lost 2-1 at the Vetch, but won the home leg 2-0 in front of an almost full house, and went on to beat Port Vale 3-0 at Wembley, where more than three quarters of the 53,471 crowd were Baggies supporters. The win meant that Albion were promoted back to Division One, along with Stoke City and Bolton Wanderers.

PORTUGAL. Albion have three times played Portuguese sides. Their first encounter was in the American-based Palo Alto end of season tournament in 1969, when a 1-0 defeat by Vitoria Setubal ended Albion's interest in winning the trophy – even though they won their next match against Edmonton All Stars, 12-0! In Albion's run to the quarter-finals of the UEFA Cup in 1978-79, they eliminated Portuguese side SC Braga in the third round, winning the first leg in Braga 2-0 and the home leg 1-0. In October 1987, assistant manager Colin Addison took the side out to Portugal for an eventful mid-season break, which included a game, which ended 1-1, against Second Division side Esperanca de Lagos. The attendance was just over 2,000, but the trip will be remembered for a brawl in a nightclub after the game, in which Albion players Tony Kelly and Don Goodman squared up to each other.

PROGRAMMES. The *Albion News* was first published by the club on Saturday, 2 September 1905, for a Second Division game with Burnley; before that date, team-sheets were given out to spectators. The programme has been published almost continuously ever since, except for a four-year break (1915-19) when only a handful of charity games were played at The Hawthorns. The large format programme (12 pages) with a classic blue cover was a great read for Albion supporters before World War Two, but paper shortages reduced the publication to a bare four pages from 1940-47. A new pocket-size format programme was issued 1947-69, when Albion moved into the vanguard of the new style 'matchday magazine' format, with a brilliant production for two seasons, 1969-71. After that, the programmes have become more and more sophisticated in terms of colour and design, but far less readable, and, as a result, less than a third of spectators are purchasing the *Albion News* (down from 67 per cent in 1987).

PROMOTION. Albion have won promotion on six occasions; five times from Division Two to One, once from what is now Division Two to the new Division One. In 1902, after being relegated the previous year for the first time ever, Albion regained their place in the top flight in style, winning 25 and drawing five of their 34 League games, ending the season as clear Champions of the Second Division. Nine years later, after a couple of near misses (one only on goal average), they were again promoted as Second Division Champions when they beat Huddersfield Town 1-0 at The Hawthorns on 29 April 1911, in front of over 30,000 spectators. After undergoing the dreaded drop again in 1927, promotion was achieved in style in 1931, when Albion achieved the unique feat of winning promotion from Division Two and winning the FA Cup in the same season, although on this occasion, for the first time, promotion was only achieved as runners-up, behind Champions Everton. Relegation came again in 1937, and World War Two intervened, and it was not until 1949 that Jack Smith, Albion's first full-time manager, took the side back onto a First Division stage, where they remained for 24 years. Once again, Albion went up as runners-up, to Champions Fulham. A 3-0 win over Leicester City at Filbert Street won Albion promotion, although a defeat two days later at Grimsby cost them the Championship. Relegated again in 1973, Johnny Giles was the successful manager in 1976, when a 1-0 win at Boundary Park, Oldham, ensured promotion for his side. This time, Albion crept up in third position, behind Sunderland and Bristol City, as the number of promotion places had been increased shortly before. Albion were relegated from the (old) First Division in 1986 and went down to the Third Division for the first time ever in 1991, although by the time that division was renamed as the Second Division, Albion were promoted again, in 1993. This time, Albion finished fourth, and, with only the top two clubs going up automatically, had to rely upon the end of season play-offs to go up, as they beat first Swansea (over two legs) and then Port Vale (who had finished four points above the Albion in third place, and who

139

would have gone up automatically themselves before the play-offs were introduced). Albion won 3-0 at Wembley, and have remained in the First Division for the past three seasons, without looking likely to try another promotion campaign for the Premiership.

Q

QUALITY GAMES. There are two games which stand out as the best displays in the Albion's history. In 1954, Albion travelled to Brussels to meet crack Hungarian side Honved, in the Le Soir Festival. Honved had seven of the Hungarian team which had so recently humiliated England by six goals to three at Wembley, including Ference Puskas, Grosics, Bozsik, Lorant, Budai, Kocsis and Czibor. Despite poor results at home before the match, Albion recovered from going a goal down to Puskas and went 3-1 ahead after an hour's play, thanks to goals from Nicholls (2) and Allen. Five minutes later, Albion's playmaker, Ray Barlow, suffered a leg injury whilst trying to prevent a breakaway goal by Czibor and Albion were reduced to ten fit men, and went down 5-3. In December 1978, buoyed by a superb 2-1 win at Highbury, Ron Atkinson took his Albion side to Old Trafford for a game which is still described by most Albion supporters as the best game they have seen. In a game that ebbed and flowed throughout, Albion pulled back from a goal down to lead 2-1, thanks to Tony Brown and Len Cantello, then went behind again, only for Tony Brown to equalise with the last kick of the first half. Albion totally controlled the second half, and added further goals from Regis and Cunningham to win 5-3, but as Ron Atkinson remarked, the scoreline did not truly represent the game; 'Goalkeeper Gary Bailey was their best player – a proper score would have been ten for us!'

QUICKEST GOALS. The fastest goal ever scored by the Albion came on 13 December 1924, after just five seconds of their home First Division game against Nottingham Forest. Albion went on to win the game 5-1, and George James scored another three to add to his rapid first goal. In November 1931, at Upton Park, W.G. Richardson scored the First Division's fastest hat-trick of all time He scored in the fifth, seventh and eighth minutes – and then added a fourth goal a minute later; four goals in the space of five minutes (although some reporters timed it as only four minutes).

R

READER, JOE. Reader was Albion's goalkeeper for 16 years, 1885 to 1901, playing in well over 500 games for the club, including the 1892 and 1895 FA Cup finals He won one England cap, and was the only Albion man to play at Four Acres, Stoney Lane and The Hawthorns. He is also the only Albion goalkeeper ever to be sent off in a first team game (at Bolton in 1895).

REGIS, CYRILLE. Cyrille Regis was born in Maripiasoula, in French Guyana. He was spotted playing for non-League Hayes by then Chief Scout Ronnie Allen, who convinced the Albion board that the young black forward was well worth £5,000. Six months later, with Allen as manager, Regis made a spectacular start to his career with two goals against Rotherham, followed by his scoring one of the best individual goals ever seen at The Hawthorns. Regis scored a number of sensational goals in the 1977-78 season, and by the time Ron Atkinson arrived as manager, he was part of a great Albion side that went so close to winning the League in 1979. Fast, skilful and powerfully built, Regis was Albion's top scorer for three successive seasons, until the arrival of Garry Thompson in 1983, turning down a £750,000 move to French side St Etienne, but was sold to Coventry in a shock move by Johnny Giles in 1984, after nearly 400 games for the Albion (140 goals), during which time he had won four full England caps.

At Coventry he won an FA Cup winners medal in 1987, later moving to Aston Villa, Wolves and Chester, after once being linked with a return to The Hawthorns under Ardiles.

RELEGATION. Albion have suffered relegation on seven occasions. As founder members of the Football League, they were relegated to Division Two for the first time in 1901, only to bounce back immediately (*see* PROMOTION). They were relegated again in 1904, and then spent six seasons in the lower division, before returning to the top flight in 1911. Relegation struck again in 1927, when the club spent another four seasons in Division Two, and again in 1938, when defeat in the last three games, all away, at Blackpool, Wolves and Middlesbrough, condemned the club to another decade out of the First Division. Promoted again in 1949, the club remained in the First Division for nearly a quarter of a century, until they finished bottom of the division in 1973, when they were relegated along with Crystal Palace. This time their stay in Division Two lasted just three years, and they remained in Division One from 1976 to 1986. The 1985-86 season was the worst in the club's history, with only four League wins being recorded all year, as Albion finished well adrift of the other relegated clubs at the bottom of the table once again. In 1991, Albion were relegated to Division Three for the first time in their history even though, for that one season only, the number of relegated clubs had been reduced to two – Albion went down with Hull City.

REYNOLDS, JOHN. Jack 'Baldy' Reynolds was a skilful half-back signed from Ulster side Distillery in 1891. In 1892, he starred in the Albion's 3-0 FA Cup final win over the Villa – three years later, he was Villa's top performer in their Cup final win over the Albion. Unusually, Reynolds won five caps for Ireland – and then another eight caps for England, making him one of the few men ever to represent two different countries. He remained at the Albion for less than two years before making a name for himself in Villa's fine Championship winning side of the 1890s, later playing for Celtic and Southampton.

RICHARDSON, WILLIAM (W.G.). William ('Ginger' – so called to distinguish him from his namesake, the Albion centre-half of

Ally Robertson

the '30s) Richardson was the finest goalscorer ever to play for the Albion. Signed from Hartlepool in 1929, he played a major part, in his first full season, in winning promotion and the FA Cup in 1931; indeed, he scored both goals in Albion's 2-1 Wembley win and scored the goal that won promotion the following week. A nimble forward with an eye for goal, W.G. scored at a rate of nearly a goal a game over his entire career – yet only managed to win one England cap in a period full of quality goalscorers, such as Dean and Camsell. He scored a club record 202 League goals for the Albion (only beaten since by Tony Brown), but also scored another 100 goals in war-time football, whilst he still holds the club's seasonal record of 40 League and Cup goals in 1935-36. He

145

played for Shrewsbury for a period immediately after the war before returning to The Hawthorns as a coach in 1947, where he remained until his death in 1959.

ROBERTS, BOB. Goalkeeper Robert Roberts holds a special position in the Albion's history in that he was the first player to be honoured by selection for the England side. West Bromwich-born, and, like many of the club's pioneers, a pupil at Christ Church School in the town and an employee at the George Salter factory which was part of the club's formation, Bob was the goalkeeper in the nascent club's first recorded game, against Hudson's on 23 November 1878 – and he kept a clean sheet in a goalless draw! (*see* FORMATION). That was before the official formation of the club, in September 1878, when the club started off under the name West Bromwich Strollers, and in the club's early days, Bob tried several outfield positions, before settling down as a goalkeeper. He certainly had the build for it – at 13 stone and standing six feet four inches, for in those early days custodians had to be pretty bulky to prevent opposing forwards taking the easy option of bundling them, and the ball, into the net to claim a goal. Roberts was Albion's goalkeeper in three successive FA Cup finals, 1886-7-8, collecting a winners' medal in the last of the three, a performance which helped to earn him three England caps. He was also Albion's goalkeeper in their first League game, at Stoke in September 1888, and he only missed three League games in the first two seasons of the new competition, before being persuaded to sign for another Albion – Sunderland Albion – at the end of the 1889-90 season. He was unhappy in the north-east, and signed back with the Albion after just one season away, but things were never the same, and after failing to displace his former deputy, Joe Reader, from the FA Cup-winning side that season (and only playing nine League games all year), he left once more, ending his career as Villa's reserve goalkeeper, and retiring after one season there, in 1893.

ROBERTSON, ALISTAIR. Ally Robertson was a typical example of the fine youth policy in operation at the Albion throughout the '60s and '70s. He made his debut against Manchester United in 1969, and by 1972 had established himself as first choice central defender, alongside John Wile – a partnership that was to last

The Robson brothers - (left to right) Justin, Gary, Bryan

until Wile's departure in 1983. Ally was an uncompromising tackler who certainly made his presence felt amongst opposition forwards; he made over 700 appearances for the club, yet mysteriously failed to win even one Scottish cap. After the arrival of Ron Saunders in 1986, he never played for the first team again, and was given a free transfer to neighbours Wolves, where he won Third and Fourth Division Championship medals as club captain, later having an unsuccessful foray into club management with Worcester City.

ROBSON, BOBBY. Originally signed as an inside forward for £20,000 from Fulham in 1956, and Albion's top scorer in 1958, Robson won 20 caps for England as a forward and later as a half-back in a marvellous career at The Hawthorns, appearing for his country in the World Cup finals of 1958 and 1962. He returned to Fulham in 1962, and was later manager at Craven Cottage for a few months, but it was as manager of the successful Ipswich side of the '70s that he really made his mark, a job which set him up for the post of England manager which he held from 1982 to

1990, when he bowed out just a missed penalty from taking England into the World Cup final. After a spell with PSV Eindhoven, Robson is now manager of Oporto.

ROBSON, BRYAN. Probably the best midfielder of the last 30 years, Bryan Robson made his Albion debut under caretaker manager Brian Whitehouse in 1975. By 1977, despite three broken legs, he had established himself as a key player in Albion's midfield, and by 1979, he was the finished article – 'Captain Fantastic' – and playing as well as any time in his career, winning the first of 90 England caps as his fine play for the Albion took the country by storm. When Ron Atkinson left The Hawthorns for Old Trafford in 1981, it was inevitable that he would return for the future England captain, and Robson left for Manchester United for a new British record fee of £1.5 million in October 1981, after more than 300 games for the Albion. With United he won winners' medals in the FA Cup (three times), the Premier League and the European Cup Winners Cup, before moving as player-manager with Middlesbrough in 1994, where his success continued with promotion at the first attempt.

ROBSON, GARY. Forever known as 'the younger brother of Bryan', it was inevitable that he would always be overshadowed by his big brother. In fact, Gary was a tough-tackling midfield grafter who was a useful player in his own right, although his very tenaciousness in the tackle meant that he, like Bryan, had long spells out with serious injury. Gary joined the Albion in July 1981, just before Bryan left for Manchester United, and remained until May 1993, his last Albion outing being as a non-playing substitute in the Wembley play-off final against Port Vale. He moved to Bradford City soon after, returning for one more game at The Hawthorns – his testimonial game – 12 months later.

ROWLEY, ARTHUR. Arthur Rowley was the greatest goalscorer the Football League has ever known, with an amazing total of 434 goals in 619 League games; four of those were for the Albion! Wolverhampton-born, Arthur failed a trial with Manchester United, but made his debut for the Old Trafford side in a War-time League game just two days after his 16th birthday. Also playing in that game was Arthur's older brother Jack, who went on to

fashion a great career with United. Surplus to United's requirements, Arthur signed for the Albion in March 1944, and scored
seven goals in nine games in the 1945-46 season. However, he
struggled to get a place in Albion League side in the Second
Division, making just 24 Second Division appearances (4 goals)
and was sold cheaply to Albion's promotion rivals, Fulham, in
December 1948. How the Albion directors must have regretted
that transfer when Rowley returned with his new side in March
1949 and scored the winner, in a snowstorm, in Fulham's 2-1 win
at The Hawthorns. Thus it was Rowley who collected a Second
Division Championship medal at the end of the season, with
Albion promoted only as runners-up. After scoring 26 goals in 56
League games for the Cottagers, Rowley moved on to Leicester
City, where he had the best days of his career, winning another
Second Divison winners' medal in 1954, and leaving Filbert
Street in 1957 with the incredible record of 251 goals in only 303
games – a good number of them against the Albion! In his best
season, 1956-57, he scored 44 goals, making him the top scorer in
the entire Football League, a feat he repeated two years later. He
moved to Shrewsbury in 1958, supposedly a spent force, yet
scored another 152 goals in 236 games at Gay Meadow before
taking over as manager, later taking similar posts at Sheffield
United and Southend United.

RUMANIA. Albion have twice met teams from Rumania. On 10
December 1958, a representative touring team from Bucharest
played one of their three games in Britain under the new
Hawthorns floodlights. The visiting squad was made up of the
best players from the CCA, Rapid, Dinamo, Stiinta and the
Progressul clubs based in Bucharest, the Rumanian capital. Albion
won the game 3-0, with goals from Forrester, Allen and Setters.
Exactly ten years later, Albion were drawn away in the first leg of
the second round of the European Cup winners leg to Dinamo
Bucharest, and they gained a 1-1 draw in what became known as
the 'Battle of Bucharest'. After Asa Hartford had given Albion a
vital away goal and early lead, Ronnie Rees retaliated to some particularly rough treatment that was being meted out by the
Rumanians, and was sent off. The incident sparked a nasty reac-
tion from the crowd, and the Albion party had to move their
bench to the edge of the pitch to escape the many rocks, bottles

and tin cans being thrown at them. At the end of the game, the Albion players huddled in the centre of the pitch until the home players were able to give them a safe escort from the pitch. Albion won the second leg 4-0, to go through 5-1 on aggregate.

RUNNERS-UP, CUP. Albion have finished as runners-up in the FA Cup on five occasions (from ten finals). They lost to Blackburn Rovers in 1886, Aston Villa in 1887 and 1895, Barnsley in 1911 and Sheffield Wednesday in 1935. They have also finished as runners-up in the League Cup twice, losing out to Queens Park Rangers in 1967 and Manchester City in 1970.

RUNNERS UP, LEAGUE. Albion have twice finished as runners-up in the First Division, in 1925, when a goalless draw in the final game at home to third placed Bolton Wanderers ensured Albion a spot behind Champions Huddersfield Town. In 1954, Albion's so-called 'Team of the Century' went so close to winning the elusive League and Cup double. After leading the First Division for almost all of the season, they won just one of their last seven games, and handed the title to neighbours Wolves, ending up in second place. In 1979, in a repeat of the 1925 scenario, Ron Atkinson's side needed a draw at home to third placed Nottingham Forest to clinch the runners-up spot, after chasing Champions Liverpool for most of the season. A late goal from million pound man Trevor Francis denied Albion runners-up spot in the First Division. Albion finished as runners-up in Division Two in 1931 (to Everton) and 1949 (to Fulham), to gain promotion to Division One.

S

SANDERS, JIM. Jim Sanders was a marvellously consistent goal-keeper who served Albion well for 13 years after World War Two. London born, he first signed as a professional for Charlton Athletic in 1941, where he joined an even greater keeper, Sam Bartram, but after being shot down with the RAF, he was invalided out of the services and told he could not play professioanl football again. However, he soon regained full mobility, and joined the Albion for a fee of £2,250 in November 1945, first appearing as a 'guest' player at the Den, and signing on full forms a few days later. Sanders was Albion's first choice goalkeeper when the Football League started up again in August 1946, until he was briefly ousted by Tom Grimley, but by the start of the 1948-49 season, he had made the position his own, and, indeed, was an ever-present during that promotion campaign. After a run of over 100 consecutive appearances, he lost his place briefly to young Norman Heath, in 1950, regained it, then fell completely out of favour, so that when manager Jack Smith was replaced by new coach Jesse Carver, Jim was very much the Albion's reserve keeper, behind Norman Heath. It was Heath who was first choice in Albion's great side which began to develop at the start of the 1952-53 season, and he played through almost all of the great games in the marvellous 1953-54 season – until he was tragically injured at Sunderland, just four days after the FA Cup semi-final against Port Vale. That injury ended Heath's career, and Sanders took full advantage of his good fortune to go on to pick up a winners' medal at Wembley in May 1954. He went on to become a fixture in the side for the next four years, in one of the most exciting sides in the country. He played nearly 400 games for the club – more than any other Albion goalkeeper until Stuart Naylor overtook his total in 1995 – until he left for Coventry City at the end of the 1957-58 season, playing his last game, and keeping a clean sheet, in a 4-0 home win against Everton in March 1958. He played just one season for Coventry (ten games), moving on to non-League Hinckley Athletic for one further season before retiring in 1960.

SANDFORD, TED. Handsworth-born Ted Sandford made his name in Albion's fine 1930-31 promotion and FA Cup winning side, as a quality inside forward. He made a second appearance at Wembley in 1935, in a nine-year stay with the club which saw him play over 300 games, originally as a forward but later as a good centre-half, and captain. He was capped once for England, leaving the Albion for Sheffield United in March 1939. Ted died in 1995.

SAUNDERS, RON. After a very successful managerial career with Norwich (promotion to Division One and League Cup finalists), Manchester City (League Cup finalists) and, particularly, Aston Villa (twice League Cup winners, First Division champions in 1981), Ron Saunders was called in by the Albion board to prune back an over-paid and ineffective playing squad in February 1986, by which time the club was effectively relegated to Division Two. The Albion failed to make any real impact in the Second Division promotion race in his only full season at the club, 1986-87, and attendances dropped alarmingly, with barely 6,000 people attending the vital relegation clash with Sunderland in April 1987. The side just escaped having to make an appearance in the Third Division play-offs at the end of that season, but when the following campaign started without a win in the first six games, including an embarrassing first-ever defeat by neighbours Walsall, in the League Cup, Saunders was dismissed in September 1987, to make way for the brief return of Ron Atkinson to The Hawthorns.

SCANDINAVIA. Albion have made several trips to Scandinavia for pre-season tours. Their very first tour outside the British Isles, in 1909, was to Sweden and Denmark, where they played Gefle, a Swedish XI, a Danish XI, plus fellow touring sides, Hull and Newcastle. Sixty years later, Albion beat Norweigian champions, SK Lyn Oslo 6-0 and lost 3-2 to a Norway Under-23 side in Bergen, whilst in 1972 they won the Orenduscupen tournament, beating Kalmaar, Helsingborg and Landskrona Bols. At the end of the successful 1978-79 season, Ron Atkinson took his team to Denmark for a three match tour against Aalborg, Fyn and IHF. In April 1981, Albion took on a full Swedish national XI and lost 2-0, whilst their last visit came in October 1984, when they drew 2-2 with Orgryte in a match to celebrate the 50th anniversary of the Swedish Pools! Albion finally met a Scandinavian side at home in 1995, when Swedish Champions IFK Gothenberg played a warm-up game at The Hawthorns to prepare for their European Champions League quarter-final. First Division Albion stunned the Swedes by winning 4-1.

SCOTLAND. Although Albion have never set out specifically on a club tour of Scotland, they have been playing sides from north of the border, home and away for around 110 years. Their first game against Scottish opponents was on 4 April 1885, when they travelled north to draw 2-2 with the Third Lanark Rifle Volunteers at their Cathkin Park ground. Two days later, they were playing again, at Four Acres, in the last game ever played at their old Four Acres ground, and it was five months later that they invited Third Lanark down to West Bromwich to officially inaugurate their new ground, Stoney Lane. Albion won that match 4-1. The following season, 1886-87, Albion beat the famed Rifle Volunteers at home and away, also fitting in a game with Hibernian on the same trip north, whilst in 1887-88, the clubs met three times, Albion winning 5-2 at home but losing twice away, 2-0 and 3-0. That was the last time that the clubs would meet, Third Lanark eventually folding in 1964. The week after that home win over the Scots, Albion went north again to meet Renton at Hampden Park, where they lost 4-1. It was to be three years before Albion played in Scotland again, when they journeyed to Heart of Midlothian's Tynecastle ground, and lost 2-0; in their last visit to Scotland for many years, the following season, they lost to Hearts once again, by a single goal. It was to be another 65 years before Albion played another Scottish side – and then it was on neutral territory, as Albion and Dundee met three times on their respective North American tours, in New York, Vancouver and Toronto, Albion winning the rubber by two games to one. The USA was again the venue the next time Albion crossed paths with a Scottish League side – in the 1966 New York Tournament – when Albion were drawn in the same league grouping as Kilmarnock, each side winning one game 2-0. In 1968-69, Albion finally got to grips with a Scottish side in a truly competitive environment – the European Cup Winners Cup, where they faced Scottish Cup holders Dunfermline Athletic at the quarter-final stage. After a goalless draw in Scotland, Albion were expected to win through in the second leg at The Hawthorns, but, in sub-zero temperatures became one of the small number of English sides to lose to Scottish rivals in Europe, 1-0 on aggregate. Seventy-seven years after their last meeting, Albion finally played the return game with Hearts, beating them 2-0 in a pre-season friendly at The Hawthorns in August 1970. Two years later, Albion played Hearts' greatest rivals, Hibernian, the Scottish Cup holders, at their Easter Road ground, in a friendly at the start of the 1972-73 season, and won 2-0. In August 1977, Albion were invited to compete in the Tennant Caledonian Cup competition, at Glasgow Rangers' Ibrox Park. In front of over 40,000 spectators, Albion beat St Mirren 4-3 in the semi-final and the following day, surprisingly, in front of 5,000 fewer fans, they beat their hosts 2-0 to win the Cup. They defended the trophy the following year, but lost on penalties to Southampton in the semi-final, then lost 2-0 to Hearts in the third place play-off game. Albion returned to Ibrox at the start of the 1983-84 season, when they lost 4-2 to Rangers in a friendly, and made their last visit across the border five years later, for a restaging (approximately) of the 1888 World Championship game, when they surprisingly lost 2-1 to lowly Dumbarton, at their Boghead ground. Albion's last game, to date, against the Scots, came in September 1994, when they beat Scottish Premier side Kilmarnock with a goal from Lee Ashcroft.

SECOND DIVISION. Albion have spent 23 seasons in the 'old' Second Division. They were first relegated to Division Two in 1901, their first season at The Hawthorns, along with fellow founder members of the Football League, Preston North End. That first campaign in the lower division was a great success, and Albion strode away with the Championship, against such sides as Glossop, Gainsborough and Burton United, losing just four games all season. Within two years, they were back again – for a much longer stay. It took Albion seven seasons of toil to win promotion again, in one of the worst periods in their history. They went close in 1906 and 1907, finishing fourth each time, but in 1909, they finished third, missing out on promotion in the very last game of the season – and then only on the smallest fraction of goal average, to Tottenham Hotspur. The following year, the club sank to its lowest League placing in its history (until finally relegated from Division Two in 1991) when they finished 11th in the division, but won promotion as Champions in 1911. There were four more seasons in the division from 1927 to 1931, until they were promoted as runners-up to Everton, the same year that they won the FA Cup; a unique record (*see* DOUBLE). Albion were once again in the lower division in 1938, where they remained until promotion in 1949. It was a quarter of a century before Albion dropped down again, staying there for three seasons until Johnny Giles won promotion for them in 1976. In 1986, Albion dropped out of the top division for the last time, and, apart from two years in the Third Division (1991-93), they have remained in what is now called the 'First Division' ever since.

SENDINGS OFF. A total of 87 players have been dismissed from the field of play whilst wearing the Albion colours. The first sending off was easily the most unbelievable – the club's greatest player, William Bassett, who was sent off in a friendly at Milwall in April 1892, for telling the referee, 'You don't understand the bally game!'. Dismissals, though, were generally a rare event in the early days of the Football League, and Albion were to have just nine more sendings off before World War Two, but they did include some of the club's most well-known players, including goalkeeper Joe Reader, sent off for retaliation in a League game at Bolton in April 1895. Mild-mannered Welsh international centre-forward Stan Davies was sent off at Bramall Lane in 1926. In September 1931, inside forward Joe Carter became the first Albion player ever to be sent off in a home game, whilst Teddy Sandford was sent off twice in two years, at Ewood Park and

White Hart Lane, with Wally Boyes the last player to be sent off before the war, at Middlesbrough in 1937. During the less competitive football played during the war, only one man was sent off playing for the Albion – but he was sent off twice in the same year. Twice in 1940, both times against Coventry City, and both times at The Hawthorns, in March and November of that year, Eddie was sent off against the 'Bantams', as they were then known, as a running feud festered across eight months and two seasons. It took another 18 years before another Albion player was dismissed, winger Derek Hogg getting his marching orders at Elland Road in December 1958, with legendary hard man Maurice Setters also going off a year later at Hillsborough. Through the '60s and '70s, dismissals increased, averaging around one per season, notable ones including sendings off at Villa Park, for fighting, for Graham Williams and Clive Clark, and on close season tour of South America and Africa, which saw Graham Lovett (against Flamengo), Graham Williams (Uganda) and Asa Hartford (East Africa) sent off, with Ronnie Rees becoming the first Albion player to go off in European competition when he retaliated against some rough treatment meted out by Dinamo Bucharest defenders in the Rumanian capital. Albion's worst offender over the years was Willie Johnston, who joined the club in 1973; he was sent off four times, against Swindon and Bristol in the Second Division, Everton in the FA Cup and Brighton in the League Cup. The 1975-76 season was a particularly bad one, with manager Johnny Giles (versus Luton), captain John Wile (Hull) and midfielder Len Cantello (Chelsea, at home) all dismissed. In 1979, Scottish forward Ally Brown recorded the second European dismissal, against Carl Zeiss Jena in the UEFA Cup, whilst in the final of a pre-season tournament in Alicante in 1977, Albion, for the first time, had two players, John Wile and Mick Martin, sent off in the same game, against Spanish side FC Hercules – and manager Ronnie Allen was also banished by the referee from the dug-out, for protesting at the decisions! Later that same season, Mick Martin was sent off again, when he became the first player since the War to be sent off in an FA Cup semi-final, Albion eventually losing 3-1 to Ipswich at Highbury. At the Victoria Ground in 1985, Jimmy Nicholl and Martyn Bennett both received red cards in a goalless draw with Stoke City. Sendings-off began to escalate rapidly in the '80s. George Reilly recorded Albion's fastest sending off when he was dismissed in a pre-season Bass Charity Vase game, against Burton Albion, after just three minutes, for head-butting. A couple of years later Carlton Palmer and Robert Hopkins were both sent off against Bradford City. The fastest sending off during an Albion career came in 1991, when on-loan defender Frank Sinclair (from Chelsea) was sent off at Exeter for head-butting the referee – in only his fourth Albion game. He never played for the club again, although defender Stacy Coldicott was not that far behind when he was sent off with just a handful of games behind him, against Torquay in an Autoglass Trophy game in 1993. In 1993, Carl Heggs became the first Albion player to go off in an Anglo-Italian game, whilst Simon Garner went close to Reilly's 'brief stay' record when he came on as a second-half substitute in the 1993-94 season's opening game, at Barnsley – and was sent off within ten minutes, for abusing a linesman. Albion have been relatively lucky over the years that very few of the dismissals really cost them anything important, the exception being the Mick Martin sending off in the 1978 FA Cup final. Just before, a Tony Brown penalty had pulled the score back to 2-1 and until the sending off, Albion looked likely to gain a replay. It was a close thing, though, in the play-off semi-final at home to Swansea in 1993. With Albion 3-2 ahead on aggregate, Mickey Mellon got himself sent off for a particularly rash challenge, and with the whole of the second half ahead, and such a narrow lead to defend, Albion's chances of reaching the Wembley final did not look particularly good. Fortunately, fate lent a hand a few minutes later, when Swansea's substitute, former Albion forward Colin West, also got himself sent off for stamping on Ian Hamilton, to level the numbers, and Albion held out to win. Albion's last sending off was Paul Mardon's last-minute dismissal in the Anglo-Italian Cup game at The Hawthorns against Reggiana in November 1995.

SETTERS, MAURICE. Maurice Setters was a classic football hard man; a tough, uncompromising wing-half who took no prisoners on the field of play. After playing ten games for his first club, Exeter City, he signed for Albion for £3,000 in January 1955, where his crude play was sharpened into something good enough to win him 16 caps for England at Under-23 level. He made his Albion debut wearing the number eight shirt, in a 1-0 defeat at

Huddersfield in December 1955; a week later, he made his home debut and scored two goals in the 4-0 defeat of Portsmouth. He played in a variety of positions whilst at The Hawthorns, including right-back, left-back (in successive games!), right- and left-half and inside-right, but he finally made the right-half position his own through most of the period 1957-59, when he displaced the ageing veteran Jimmy Dudley. He was sold to Manchester United, for £30,000, after 120 League appearances for the Albion. In his five years at Old Trafford Setters won an FA Cup winners medal, in 1963, and played nearly 200 games for United, before moving down the road to Stoke, then finished off his playing career with spells at Coventry City and Charlton. He was manager at Doncaster Rovers for three years, 1971-74, then moved to Sheffield Wednesday as coach under Jack Charlton, who he teamed up with again in 1986, when he became assistant manager of the Republic of Ireland international side until Charlton's resignation in 1995.

SHINTON, FRED. Albion supporters never really saw the best of Wednesbury-born centre-forward Fred Shinton – but what they saw was good enough! He was only at The Hawthorns for a little over two years, but he scored 50 goals in less than 70 games. He had an eye for goal, scoring four hat-tricks (three 'fours' and a treble) in the space of 13 games in 1906, and finishing as the club's top scorer with 28 goals in just 30 games. Sold to Leicester Fosse in December 1907, Shinton was out of the game by 1912, forced to retire on medical grounds at the age of 29.

SIMMONS, 'CHIPPY'. As well as Fred Shinton, Albion were blessed with another quality goalscorer at around the same time – Charlie 'Chippy' Simmons. West Bromwich born, Simmons first signed for the club in 1898, when he partnered Billy Bassett. He was the club's top scorer in the Second Division Championship season of 1901-02, but moved to Southern League West Ham for one season in 1904, returning to the Albion a year later for another two seasons when he successfully linked up with Shinton – the two men scored 34 goals between them in 1905-06. Simmons left for Chesterfield in March 1907, after 200 games for the Albion.

Richard Sneekes

SIMOD CUP. The Simod Cup was the first sponsored title for the Full Members Cup, for the seasons 1987-88 and 1988-89. Albion won one (3-0 at Oldham) and lost two (2-1 at Ipswich and 5-2 at West Ham) of their three games in the competition. For the 1989-90 season, the computer company Zenith Data Systems took over the sponsoring of the competition.

SMITH, JACK. Jack Smith had three distinctly separate spells connected with West Bromwich Albion. He was an unsuccessful trialist as a left-back at The Hawthorns in the '20s, at the age of 16, before signing as a professional for Wolverhampton Wanderers. During World War Two, whilst a Chelsea player, he made more than 60 appearances guesting for the Albion in wartime football, his playing career ending prematurely when a tram ran over his foot in Wolverhampton. His third spell was the more significant; in July 1948, Smith was nominated as Albion's first genuine team manager (*see* EVERISS, FRED) when the former secretary-manager post was divided into two. In his first season, he took Albion back into the First Division, where they struggled to hold their own for some time before his dismissal (according to the Albion at the time – his resignation!) in April 1952. Although Albion rarely reached the heights during his four-year spell at The Hawthorns, Smith was responsible for bringing a number of important players to the club, such as Stan Rickaby, George Lee, Johnny Nicholls and Ronnie Allen, who were to provide the basis of the club's success in the latter part of the '50s.

SNEEKES, RICHARD. The 27-year-old Dutchman was Alan Buckley's biggest-ever signing when he moved to The Hawthorns from Bolton in March 1996 – but with a 'get-out' clause in his contract should the Albion be relegated. With 22 Youth and two Under-21 caps for Holland, Sneekes was a product of the famous Ajax nursery – and in fact, was the youngest player ever to appear for the Amsterdam side – but fell out of favour and was sold to Fortuna Sittard, and then on to Bolton Wanderers. A class midfield player, he became the first Albion midfielder ever to score in his first three games for the club, making a fine debut in the 4-4 draw with Watford.

SOUTH AMERICA. Albion went on a tour of South America in 1966, when they played six games right across the continent.

Date	Opponent	Score
13 May	Alianza Lima	3-2
15 May	Sporto Cristal (Peru)	2-1
22 May	Uruguay Select	1-1
25 May	Newells Old Boys (Argentina)	0-0
29 May	Uruguay Select	0-2
5 June	Flamengo (Brazil)	2-1

SPAIN. Always the most popular destination for pre-season tournaments, Albion first travelled to Spain for a testimonial game against Athletico Bilbao in 1958, a trip they repeated in 1971. In 1977, they competed in the Costa Blanca Tournament, finishing as runners-up to FC Hercules in a game which saw two Albion players dismissed. Two years later, Albion were invited to the prestigious Trofeo Teresa Tournament in La Coruna, but missed the chance of playing against Laurie Cunningham's Real Madrid when they lost to Sporting Gijon and Honved. In 1981, Albion won the Seville Tournament, beating Real Betis and Seville, but the following year finished as wooden spoonists in the Barcelona tournament, losing to Espanol and Osasuna. In 1989, Albion lost 6-1 to Real Madrid in the San Jose Cup in the USA. Albion's best victory over a Spanish side came in the UEFA Cup in 1978, when they beat a star-studded Valencia, including Argentinian World Cup star, Mario Kempes, 3-1 on aggregate.

STAFFORDSHIRE CUP. The Staffordshire Football Association was created in 1877, and the Staffordshire Cup was instigated the following season. Albion first entered in the 1882-83 season – and won the competition at the first attempt! Their first tie was away to Bloxwich Strollers in November 1882, and they went on to beat them after a replay, also accounting for Aston Villa (the first-ever meeting between the two clubs), Birmingham St George's (with whom they drew 2-2, but who were subsequently disqualified for fielding two ineligible players) and Leek White Star (beaten 8-0 in the semi-final). The final was held, as usual, at the Victoria Ground, Stoke, against the home side, but Albion, against all the odds, won 3-2 to collect the first trophy in the club's history. The following year, Albion again reached the final, at the same venue, but lost 2-1 to the Birmingham St George side, but won the Cup again in 1886 (beating Stoke 4-2 in a replay at Stoney Lane) and 1887 (beating Walsall Swifts at the Victoria Ground). In 1888, Wolves prevented the Staffs Cup 'hat-trick' by beating the Albion in a second replay, again at Stoney Lane. As a Football League club, Albion again won the Cup in 1889, beating Leek 2-0 at Stoke, but then failed to reach the final again for another nine years, when they lost 1-0 at Stoke to Burslem Port Vale in 1898. They gained their revenge in 1900, beating Burslem 5-0 in a final replay at Aston (after a 1-1 draw at Stoke) and two years later beat Stoke 3-0 in the final at Burslem. Albion's last appearance for the first team in the final of the Staffs Cup came in November 1902 when, as in their first final, they beat Stoke, this time by two goals to nil at Aston, the 10,000 attendance being a record for a Staffs Cup final involving Albion. Three years later, as with the other local Cup competitions, the Staffordshire Cup was downgraded to permit League clubs' reserve sides to enter. Albion's reserve side won the Cup again in 1924, 1926, 1932 and 1933 and, after a long break from the competition, shared it with Stoke City in 1969. Although Albion have not entered a team in the Staffs Cup since that date, Stoke and Port Vale still enter their reserves sides, much as Albion do in the Birmingham Senior Cup.

STATHAM, DEREK. Derek Statham got his Albion career off to the best possible start when, playing at left-back at the Victoria Ground against Stoke City, in December 1976, he scored a wonderful solo goal against Peter Shilton. Despite being the best full-back of the period, he only won three England caps because he could not dislodge the consistent Kenny Samson, but he was a marvellously consistent performer himself for the Albion, in a career dogged by injury. In 1987, after 12 years at The Hawthorns, a deal was arranged with Liverpool, but they pulled out of the move after a medical, Statham later moving to Southampton, then Stoke, and he finished his career with Walsall and Telford United.

STILES, NOBBY. World Cup winner Nobby Stiles did not want the position as Albion manager in October 1985 – but then again, who would have? He had been brought in as youth team manager by his brother-in-law, Johnny Giles, in February 1984, as one third of the 'A-Team', along with Giles' ex-Leeds team-mate, Norman Hunter. When Giles resigned after a club record run of nine successive League defeats in October 1985, Stiles grudgingly took over the position of boss of bottom placed Albion, and took them to their first win of the season – in their 13th game! There was a noticeable improvement in results under Stiles, who had previously taken Preston to promotion in his first managerial position, but he gladly handed over the reins to incoming boss Ron Saunders in February 1986, by which time Albion were virtually doomed to relegation anyway. Stiles returned to coaching the youth side until Brian Talbot replaced him with Cyril Lea in 1989, when he took up a similar post at Old Trafford.

SUBSTITUTES. Albion's first substitute in a League game was Graham Lovett, who replaced Ken Foggo in the 4-3 win at Northampton in September 1965. In the FA Cup final against Everton in May 1968, Dennis Clarke became the first substitute to appear in an FA Cup final, when he replaced John Kaye for the 30 minutes of extra time.

SWITZERLAND. Albion have thrice played Swiss sides. In October 1959, as one of a series of 'Floodlit Continental Friendlies' they drew 0-0 at The Hawthorns with Swiss Cup holders Grenchen. Twenty-one years later, Albion competed in a pre-season tournament in Split, Yugoslavia, where, after losing their first game to their hosts, Hadjuk Split, they met Swiss side FC Zurich in a consolation game, and drew 0-0. The following season, in the UEFA Cup, Albion were drawn against Zurich Grasshoppers, who had won the Swiss League a record 17 times – and the Cup 13 times; another record. Yet Albion were expected to win comfortably, so it was quite a surprise when they lost the first leg 1-0 in Zurich. It was even more of a surprise when the Swiss won 3-1 at The Hawthorns. That game was Albion's last in 'proper' (i.e. excluding the Anglo-Italian Cup) European competition.

T

TALBOT, BRIAN. The signing of Brian Talbot was a masterstroke by manager Ron Atkinson in January 1988, his midfield energy helping to keep the club out of the Third Division that season. When Atkinson abruptly left to manage Athletico Madrid in October 1988, Talbot took over as player-manager on a caretaker basis, being given the job in his own right after five successive wins. Within two months, Albion had moved from the bottom to the top of the table, but injuries meant that the side just missed out on the play-offs. The following season, Talbot abandoned his usual passing game and reverted to a long ball ploy – by 1991, Albion had been beaten 4-2 at home to non-League Woking in the FA Cup, and were struggling in the League, and Talbot was dismissed.

TALBUT, JOHN. Jimmy Hagan signed experienced centre-half Talbut from Burnley for £30,000 in December 1966, to help shore up a defence that was leaking goals alarmingly, and by the end of the season the England Under-23 international had displaced Albion stalwart centre-half Stan Jones. Talbut was spared the indignity of the defeat by Queens Park Rangers at Wembley in the League Cup final, because he was Cup-tied, and he was an ever-present in the Albion defence for the next two seasons, as he went on to win an FA Cup winners medal, as well as a loser's tankard in the 1970 League Cup final. Strong in the air, although

Brian Talbot

a little suspect on the ground, Talbut was a useful centre-half who played nearly 200 games for the club, his only goal coming against AS Roma in the 1970 Anglo-Italian tournament. His days were numbered, however, when Alan Ashman signed John Wile from Peterborough United in December 1970. Talbut never played for the League side again, moving to Belgium at the end of that season as player-manager to KV Mechelen, a Belgian Second Division club whom Albion played on their tour of Belgium in 1974.

TAYLOR, BOB. Bob Taylor was signed by Bobby Gould for a bargain £300,000 from Bristol City in January 1992, as a belated replacement for top scorer Don Goodman, whose sale had been forced on Gould by his directors three months before. Albion won just three out of the 11 games played between Goodman's departure and Taylor's arrival, at a period of great unrest by the supporters, but the side improved straightaway, with Taylor scoring the opening goal on his debut in a 2-0 home win against Third Division leaders Brentford. The former Leeds United apprentice

Bob Taylor

finished the season with eight goals from 19 games, but it was under new manager Ossie Ardiles that his Albion career really flourished, and he became the first Albion player for over 70 years to score as many as 37 goals in a season (in all competitions), matching a similar record with Bristol City in their promotion season three years earlier. His strengths are difficult to pinpoint; although the striker lacks a certain amount of pace, he makes up for it with great strength on the ball and a very high work-rate, with a marvellous ability to hit the back of the net. Back in the First Division, and as at City, Taylor's goal-scoring became a little more erratic, although, after a poor start, he still reached the 21-

goal mark in 1993-94. However, the following season, his tally had dropped as low as seven, with Andy Hunt usurping him as Albion's top scorer, and his very presence at the Albion became a topic for debate, as Coventry City came in with a £1.5 million bid for the centre-forward after Alan Buckley had taken over. Buckley rejected the bid, and Taylor played his part in keeping the club in the First Division the following year. In December 1995, Sheffield United's new manager, Howard Kendall, made another £1 million plus bid for the striker, which the Albion board actually accepted, but this time the player himself declined the move, with the Blades stuck in the bottom three of the First Division at the time.

TEN MEN. Albion have finished many games with only ten men, because of injury or dismissal, and, indeed, in the 1957-58 season, they made a point of winning games, especially in the FA Cup, win a man short, most notably 5-1 at Nottingham Forest, and 4-1 at home to Sheffield United, in successive rounds of the Cup. However, only once have Albion actually started a game with only ten men; at Everton in September 1894. William Richards failed to make the train to Liverpool, and Albion played the whole game with ten men, losing 4-1. Richards was subsequently suspended and fined one guinea, although with the team struggling to score goals, he was back in the side within six weeks.

TEST MATCHES. For many years after the formation of the Second Division in 1892, the bottom two clubs of the First Division were obliged to play in a series of Test matches against the top two clubs from the lower division, to decide relegation. In 1895, Albion escaped the Test matches by winning their last game against Sheffield Wednesday by the required six goals to nil, but there was no escape the following year.

A	Manchester City	1-1
H	Manchester City	6-1
A	Liverpool	2-0
H	Liverpool	2-0

Albion finished second in the 'mini-division', behind Liverpool, and so remained in the First Division.

TESTIMONIALS. Albion, particularly in the last century, and, more recently, during Ron Atkinson's period as manager, have played a large number of testimonial matches at grounds across the world as benefit matches for players as a reward for long service, or because their careers had been terminated by injury. Norman Heath, Graham Williams, Bobby Cram, Bobby Hope, Tony Brown, Jeff Astle, Ray Wilson, Johnny Giles, John Osborne, Len Cantello, John Wile, Alistair Robertson (twice), Brendan Batson, Tony Godden, Martyn Bennett, Gary Robson and Stuart Naylor have all been granted testimonial games at The Hawthorns.

TEXACO CUP. The Texaco Cup was the second sponsored competition sanctioned by the Football League, following the success of the pre-season Watney Cup. The giant multi-national oil conglomerate ploughed £100,000 into the competition in 1970, with the 16 competing clubs from England, Scotland, Eire and Ulster each receiving £1,000, with the eventual finalists sharing £7,000 in prize-money. Albion lost both legs of their first round tie to Greenock Morton, 2-1 in Scotland, 1-0 at The Hawthorns. In 1972-73, Albion again entered the Texaco Cup, which was now becoming an Anglo-Scottish competition, the Troubles in Ireland forcing the Irish sides from both sides of the border to withdraw. Albion beat Sheffield United 1-0 at The Hawthorns with an injury time goal from striker Bobby Gould, after a 1-1 draw at Bramall Lane. In the second round, Albion beat Newcastle United 2-1 in the home leg, but lost 3-1 at Tynecastle to lose 4-3 on aggregate. Newcastle went on to beat Burnley in the first all-English final. By 1974-75, the English section of the Texaco Cup was played as a series of pre-season qualifying groups, the four group winners meeting four invited Scottish clubs in the quarter-finals. Albion failed to qualify, beating Norwich 5-1, drawing 0-0 with Birmingham, and losing 2-1 at Peterborough. Newcastle beat Southampton in the final to retain the trophy. In 1975, Texaco ended their sponsorship, and the competition continued as the Anglo-Scottish Tournament.

THIRD DIVISION. The Third Division (South) was formed in 1920, with the Northern Section following 12 months later. Until May 1991, Albion were one of just a dozen top clubs who had never lost their full membership of the Football League, i.e. had never played below the top two divisions. However, a 1-1 draw against Bristol Rovers at Twerton Park on the final day of the 1990-91 season was enough to send Albion down to Division Three, despite an unbeaten run of nine games under new manager Bobby Gould. Albion won their first-ever game in Division Three, 6-3, at home to Exeter City, and went on to head the table, but ultimately missed the play-offs by finishing in ninth place – the lowest placing in the club's history. The following season, the breakaway of the Premier League meant that the division was renamed Division Two – and Albion won promotion by finishing fourth, and beating Port Vale 3-0 at Wembley.

THOMPSON, GARRY. Garry Thompson was a powerful, athletic centre-forward signed by Ron Wylie from his former club Coventry City in February 1983. He only played just over 100 games for the Albion, but scored at a rate of a goal every other game, briefly partnering Cyrille Regis in a twin centre-forward formation that struck terror into the hearts of First Division defences; Regis was majestic on the ground, Thompson unbeatable in the air. He was sold to Sheffield Wednesday at the start of the 1985-86 season, and Albion, lacking any height or weight up front, never recovered, and were relegated at the end of the season. He later played for Aston Villa, Watford, Cardiff and Northampton Town.

TRANSFERS, RECORD. The most Albion have paid for a player is £748,000 for Peter Barnes – way back in 1979. The most Albion have received for a player was £1.5 million from Manchester United – a new British record at the time – for Bryan Robson in October 1981.

TREWICK, JOHN. 'Tucka' Trewick was a product of Albion's excellent scouting system in the north-east, arriving at The Hawthorns at the same time as Bryan Robson. A useful midfield player, although lacking a little pace, John remained at the Albion from 1974 until his transfer to Newcastle United in 1980. Later he had spells with Oxford United (winning Second Division Championship and League Cup medals) and Birmingham City, before returning to football as Albion's Football in the

169

Community Officer in 1993, later moving up to take over the management of the reserve side under Keith Burkinshaw. He is now a first team coach at The Hawthorns under Alan Buckley.

U

UEFA CUP. Three times Albion qualified for the UEFA Cup between 1978 and 1981. In 1978-79, they beat Galatasaray, Braga, and Valencia before losing to Red Star Belgrade in the quarter-finals. The following season, they lost in the first round to Carl Zeiss Jena, of East Germany, and suffered a similar early exit, to Grasshoppers of Zurich, in 1981-82.

UNITED COUNTIES LEAGUE. The United Counties League was concocted to fill out fixture lists for the 1893-94 season, competed for ostensibly by the best sides of the counties of Staffordshire, Warwickshire, Derbyshire, Nottinghamshire and Yorkshire. Albion were grouped in the southern section, along with Stoke, Wolves, Aston Villa and Second Division runners-up Small Heath, until Villa dropped out at the last minute. The initial stages were played on a home and away basis, and Albion won their group with four wins and two defeats from their six games. In the northern group, Derby County came out on top in front of Notts County, Nottingham Forest and the two Sheffield clubs, and entertained Albion in the final at Derby's Racecourse Ground on 30 April 1894. The game finished 1-1, after extra time, and the decision was made, there and then, to share the trophy for six months each. However, at the start of the following season, it was decided, for financial reasons, to disinter the competion, and the match was replayed – again at Derby – on 6 October 1894, and Albion lost 2-1 in front of less than 6,000 fans. Derby were the first – and last – winners of the competition.

USA, TOURS. Albion have played in the United States five times. They first toured North America in 1958, and they played one game in the USA, at Ebbetts Field, New York, on 24 May of that year. It was an exhibition game, against another touring side, Dundee, and ended in a 2-2 draw. In July 1966, Albion competed in the New York International Tournament, in the same group as Kilmarnock, Ferencvaros and Polonia Bytom, but only won one of their six games and failed to qualify for the finals. In May 1969, Albion again toured the USA and Canada, playing four games in the Palo Alto Tournament in California, in which they met Dukla Prague, California Clippers, Vitoria Setubal and Edmonton All Stars, beating the latter 12-0. Ron Atkinson's last games in charge of the Albion were on the club's American tour of 1981; two games were played in Canada, with a brief excursion south of the border to beat NASL side Portland Timbers 1-0. Albion's last trip to the States was in 1990, for the San Jose Cup. They lost 6-1 to Real Madrid in the semi-final, then lost 4-2 to Brazilian side Vasco da Gama to end up with the wooden spoon. To finish off the tour, Albion played – and beat – two college sides, Arizona Condors and Los Angeles Heat.

USA, ALBION PLAYERS IN. The North American Soccer League (NASL) was formed in 1966, and lasted 19 years, and although hardly a success in domestic terms, it proved to be a haven for British football stars looking for well-paid temporary work during the summer months. The first Albion player to go out to the NASL was full-back Bobby Cram, who had been released by the Albion immediately after his testimonial match in 1967. He was a regular for Vancouver Royals 1967-9, before returning to England to play for the famous giant-killing Colchester United side of the early '70s. He later returned to the NASL, playing another five games for Seattle Sounders in 1974. Also on the Seattle roster at that time was a young forward, David Butler, who had been released by the Albion without making the first team – he went on to make a good career for himself with Seattle and Portland Timbers. Other Albion players who had been released early by the Albion, and went on to play regularly in the USA include full-back Roger Minton (Washington Diplomats), Alan Merrick (Minnesota Kickers), Russell Allen, son of Ronnie (Chicago Sting), Trevor Thompson (Washington) and Wayne Hughes (Tulsa). Other former Albion players who moved to the USA at the end of their careers include Bobby Hope (Philadelphia and Dallas), Willie Johnston (Vancouver), Ray Treacy (Toronto Tornados), Tony Brown (New England and Jacksonville) and Johnny Giles (Philadelphia), although Giles later became coach of Vancouver Whitecaps. Albion players who interrupted their Albion careers for temporary football in America include Ally Brown (Portland 1981), John Wile (Vancouver 1982) and Len Cantello (Dallas 1978). In 1984, Albion made their first signing from the USA when they bought Carl Valentine from Vancouver Whitecaps – two years later, he returned to finish his career in the USA and Canada.

USSR, TOUR. Albion toured the Soviet Union in June 1957, when they became the first British side to win on the other side of the Iron Curtain. Their first match was at Zenit Leningrad where they drew 1-1 in front of 80,000 spectators. They then flew to Georgia, where they beat Dinamo Tblisci 3-1, finishing off in Moscow by beating the crack Russian Army side, CDSA, 4-2, in front of another massive crowd. Derek Kevan was the hero of the tour, with five goals, his bustling style being much appreciated by the Russians. In October 1957, Albion played host to CDSA Moscow to inaugurate their new floodlights, and won 6-5. Albion last played a side from the Soviet Union as part of their pre-season warm-up in 1986, when Russian Cup holders Torpedo Moscow won 2-0 at The Hawthorns.

V

VALENTINE, CARL. Manchester-born Valentine began his career with Oldham Athletic in 1976, playing nearly 100 games before moving to Canada, with Vancouver Whitecaps, where he became a naturalised Canadian, and formed a useful partnership with Peter Beardsley which helped the Whitecaps win the Soccer Bowl in 1979. As the NASL was folding, Valentine was brought back to England for £60,000 by Albion manager Johnny Giles, Vancouver's former coach, and he made a calamitous debut at Ipswich in October 1984, never adjusting to the fast pace, and going off injured after just 25 minutes. He stayed at the Albion until January 1986 season, playing just 44 times in the League (six goals) and never really caught the eye as a winger, lacking pace and some elementary skills, although his slighty fortunate winner against local rivals Aston Villa in April 1985 did help to endear him to the Albion fans to some extent. In 1985, Valentine became the first Albion player to win a Canadian international cap when he made his debut for his adopted country in a vital World Cup qualifying game against Honduras – Canada won the game and Carl went on to represent them in their first appearance in the World Cup finals in Mexico in 1986. On leaving the Albion, Valentine played for North American sides Wichita, Cleveland and Calgary.

VERNON, JACK. Jack Vernon was the second of Fred Everiss' canny Irish scoops just after World War Two, following on from centre-forward Dave Walsh. Vernon was a cool, polished centre-half, good in the air and masterful on the ground, who was signed for an Albion record transfer fee of nearly £10,000, from Belfast Celtic, in the middle of the harsh winter of 1946-47 – so bad that the player had to wait five weeks to make his debut. After taking a little while to settle in to the faster pace of English football, Vernon was acknowledged as one of the finest centre-backs in the country, being selected for the Great Britain side which met the Rest of the World side at Hampden Park in 1947. He won 22 caps for Northern Ireland and the Republic of Ireland – most as captain – and skippered the Albion to promotion in 1949. Vernon left the Albion in 1952, with the Albion continuing to pay him a salary for a further two years, as he continued to play part-time football with Crusaders of Belfast, whilst running his family's butchery business in the city.

VICTORIES IN SEASON, MOST AND LEAST. Albion won 28 matches (from 42 games) in their Championship season of 1919-20, which is their best ever performance. Their worst performance was in 1985-86, when they were relegated from the First Division with just four wins all season in the League.

VIDEOS. Two videotapes have been issued by the club: *Backstage* (1991) and *The Official History* (1993), but they are of variable quality. There are also two compilations, not issued by the club, featuring games culled from ATV's *Star Soccer* programme, of Albion's best matches during the '70s — these are well worth having, featuring the wins at Manchester United (5-3), Wolves (3-0) and at home to Spurs (4-2) and Liverpool (2-0). A BBC *Match of the Day* compilation was scheduled for 1991, but has been put on hold indefinitely.

W

WALES. Albion's first trip to play a match in the Principality was on Boxing Day 1882, when they won 5-2 at Acton Park, the home of Wales' oldest football club, Wrexham, and they won the return home game 3-1 later in the season. In January 1884 came Albion's first competitive match with a Welsh side, when the famous Druids came to the Four Acres. They arrived late, and the referee allowed Albion to kick off without them! The Albion players went through the formality of netting the ball, so as to claim the match, but shortly afterwards the Druids, delayed by a late train, turned up, and insisted the match go ahead. Albion scored another legitimate goal, winning the fourth round tie 1-0. In 1890, Albion again crossed Offa's Dyke to play at Chirk, the holders of the Welsh Cup, who were beaten 5-1, and Albion won the return match, played the following season, 3-0. Albion's record against the Welsh continued to flourish, as they won 3-1 at Wrexham in 1892, 2-0 in 1895, and then won 8-2 at Aberystwyth, also in 1895. Later the same year, they returned to Aberystwyth and won 10-1, then won 2-1 at Llandudno in 1896, 1-0 at Chirk again, in 1898 and surpassed themselves in 1899 with an amazing 13-1 win at Swansea Town (no connection with the current Swansea City club). Albion first met a Welsh side in the Football League as recently as October 1921, when they drew 2-2 with Cardiff City in a First Division game at The Hawthorns, losing 2-0 in their first visit to Ninian Park a week later. Albion first met the present-day Swansea side when relegated to Division Two in 1927, and lost 6-1 at the Vetch Field in February 1929, Albion's heaviest defeat against a Welsh side. Albion's third round FA Cup defeat at Swansea in 1987 was the first time that they had lost to a Fourth Division side in the competition. In May 1930, Albion played Cardiff City in a charity match for the Montgomeryshire Hospital Fund, at Newtown, winning 2-1, and have also played several testimonial games at Swansea, in 1971 (for ex-Albion man Walter Robbins), 1977 (for former Albion goalkeeper Tony Millington) and 1986 (to raise cash to keep Swansea City in business). Albion met the now defunct Newport County for one League season in 1946-47, in Division Two, winning 7-2 at Somerton Park. Nearly 40 years later, they made their last visit to the ground (now no longer in existence) to lose 2-1 in the John Relish testimonial match. Albion have still to play Wrexham in a League game, but in 1930, they lost 1-0 to the Third Division side in the third round of the FA Cup, then returned to the Racecourse Ground 40 years later to win 2-1 in the first round of the sponsored Watney Cup.

WALSH, DAVID. David Walsh, Albion's first signing after the Second World War, started his Football League career in spectacular style, scoring in his first six games for the Albion – a new club record – after signing from Irish side Linfield for £3,500 in May 1946. Walsh was a sturdy, powerful centre-forward, whose 70 goals the previous season for Linfield and Ireland had attracted Albion's interest in a forward to replace the ageing W.G. Richardson. Walsh remained at The Hawthorns for nearly five years, winning 20 caps for the Republic of Ireland – and 11 caps for Northern Ireland! He scored exactly 100 goals for the Albion, in just under 200 games, before leaving for Aston Villa for £25,000 in December 1950, after the arrival of his eventual successor, Ronnie Allen.

WARTIME FOOTBALL. Albion were one of the few professional clubs to refuse to compete in the various Regional Football Leagues during World War One, instead opting just to play a handful of fund-raising games against the other Midlands clubs. In total, including a Midland Victory League competition, organised in April 1919, Albion played just two dozen matches between April 1915 and August 1919. Things were very much different during World War Two. The normal League campaign was abandoned on Sunday, 3 September, after Germany's invasion of Poland, with just four games played – those results were expunged from the League's records and, after six weeks' delay, Albion competed with Wolves, Birmingham, Walsall and Northampton, amongst others, in the Midland Regional League. Aston Villa were notable by their absence, as they decided not to enter organised competitions for the first three years of the war. In all, over the six years of the war, Albion played over 300 games in the Midland, North and South Leagues, as well as their ancillary cup competitions, although, with many players unavailable in the forces, standards were low – and attendances were lower, with several matches at The Hawthorns, in the early days of the war, failing to reach four figures. In 1944, Albion won the Midland Cup, beating Nottingham Forest 6-5 on aggregate over two legs. In 1945-46, Albion finished fourth in a very competitive Football League South, which included Aston Villa, Champions Birmingham, Arsenal, Chelsea and Tottenham. In that 'transitional' season, the Football Association also reintroduced the FA Cup, but with every round up to the quarter-final stage being played over two legs, for the one and only time in the competition's history. Albion beat Cardiff City 5-1 on aggregate in the third round, but lost 4-1 to Derby in the fourth.

WARTIME INTERNATIONALS. A Victory International was played at The Hawthorns on 20 October 1945, when more than 54,000 people filled the ground to see Wales beat England in what is classed as an 'unofficial' international. Albion's Harry Kinsell was in the England side at left-back.

WATNEY CUP. The Watney Cup was the first sponsored tournament endorsed by the Football League. It was a pre-season knockout, open to the top goal-scoring clubs in each division from the previous season, excluding those clubs who had won trophies, promotion or had qualified for Europe. Albion qualified in its second season, in August 1971, and won at Wrexham and Halifax to reach the final, against Fourth Division giant-killers Colchester (who had sensationally beaten Leeds United in the FA

Cup a few months before). Nearly 20,000 people (and the *Match of the Day* cameras) saw a thrilling game at The Hawthorns – new manager Don Howe's first home game in charge – which ended 4-4. The Essex side won 4-3 in what was Albion's first-ever penalty shoot-out.

WEDNESBURY OLD ATHLETIC. Wednesbury Old Athletic – the 'Old 'Uns' – were formed four or five years before the Albion and by 1877 they were acclaimed as the West Midlands' top club, when they were the first winners of the Birmingham Senior Cup. It was to be another seven years before the two clubs met, with the Athletic showing they were still a force to be reckoned with when they beat Albion 5-2 at Four Acres. But Wednesbury were a declining force, and it was soon to be Albion who were to challenge Aston Villa for supremacy in the region, with Albion's most important victory against the Wednesbury side coming in the FA Cup in November 1885, when the Old 'Uns let slip a two goal lead, Albion winning the second round 3-2 to go on to become the first Midlands side to reach the FA Cup final. Albion were one of the beneficiaries when WOA closed in 1893 and they signed the Athletic's most famous player, West Bromwich-born England international George Holden, who won his caps whilst playing for Wednesbury OA. By the time he moved to the Albion, however, in 1886, he was past his best, and only played in the first four games of Albion's run to their second successive FA Cup final in 1887. He returned to Athletic later that year.

WEDNESBURY TOWN. Wednesbury Town were the oldest football club in neighbouring Wednesbury, founded in 1873 and Wednesbury FC. Although not a great club by any means, they were Albion's first-ever FA Cup opponents, at Albion's Four Acres ground on 10 November 1883. Although Albion were expected to win, Town pulled off a shock 2-0 victory.

WEMBLEY. Albion have appeared at the Empire Stadium on seven occasions since Wembley was built for the Empire Exhibition in 1923 – and they have a curious record of winning on every other trip they make there! Thus they won against Birmingham in their first visit in 1931 – and with it the unique double of FA Cup and promotion from the Second Division – but lost the FA Cup final

, to Sheffield Wednesday four years later. In 1954, they won the FA Cup for a fourth time, 3-2 against Preston North End – but lost there to Third Division Queens Park Rangers in the 1967 League Cup final. Twelve months later, they were back again, and they beat Everton 1-0, after extra time, to win the FA Cup again. In 1970, it was the League Cup final, when they lost 2-1 to Manchester City, but won 3-0 there in 1993, in the Second Division play-off final against Port Vale. Don't put your money on an Albion win the next time they get to Wembley!

WILE, JOHN. John Wile was manager Alan Ashman's last major signing for the Albion. He had spotted the centre-half's potential in a League Cup defeat at Peterborough United, when the former Sunderland apprentice had completely blotted out Albion's star centre-forward, Jeff Astle. In December 1970, Wile signed for Albion for £32,000, as a replacement for the out of favour John Talbut, and from that date on Wile was a virtual fixture in the Albion line-up, usually as captain, as he played exactly 500 League games before his return to Peterborough as player-manager in 1983. In all competitions, Wile played in over 700 games for the Baggies, seven times playing every match in a season, usually alongside another great stalwart, Alistair Robertson. He was a dominating, assertive defender, superb in the air, if a little lacking on the ground, but, with the exception perhaps of Malcolm MacDonald, was rarely given the runaround by an opposing centre-forward. A famous photograph from Wile's 12 years at the club – he was awarded a testimonial game in 1982 – was that from the 1978 FA Cup semi-final against Ipswich, which showed him with a bandage around his head, his Albion shirt soaked in blood after a terrible clash of heads with Ipswich's Brian Talbot (another future Albion captain). Despite his terrible injury, Wile insisted in carrying on until virtually forced from the field by manager Ron Atkinson. Wile did not have great success with Peterborough, and retired from playing in 1986 to pursue a career in sports management.

WILLIAMS, GRAHAM. Welshman Graham Williams came up through the Albion's youth team set-up as a left winger, but was soon converted to left-back where he took over in the first team from his namesake and countryman, Stuart Williams, although

John Wile (left) and Derek Statham

both men shared the two full-back positions on occasions for both club and country. Eighteen years with the Albion, Williams played nearly 400 games for the club, being granted a testimonial game in 1966, captaining his side to success in both the League Cup final of 1966 and the FA Cup final two years later. He was capped 26 times by Wales. Williams was released by his former right-back partner, manager Don Howe, in 1972, taking over Weymouth as player-manager, later coaching in Greece, Kuwait and, for three months, as 'chief coach/manager' at Cardiff City.

WILLIAMS, STUART. Stuart Williams, son of a Wrexham director, was the most capped of all Albion's international players, win-

Graham Williams with the League Cup, 1966

ning 33 of his 43 caps for Wales whilst at The Hawthorns. He joined the Albion groundstaff in November 1950 and stayed at the club for 12 years, initially, rather unsuccessfully, as an inside forward, but mainly as a fine full-back in nearly 300 games for the club. He was particularly unlucky in 1954 when, according to some versions of the official Cup final programme, he was down to replace injury victim Stan Rickaby for the final against Preston. Instead, at the last minute, manager Vic Buckingham decided to bring in an out-of-position Joe Kennedy instead. Williams was dismissed by the Albion in September 1962, moving to Southampton for £15,000, and he made another 200 or so appearances at The Dell before returning to the Albion as trainer in time for the 1968 FA Cup final. Other coaching jobs followed at Aston Villa, Southampton and Stavanger, in Norway.

WILSON, JOE. Charlie 'Tug' Wilson came to the attention of manager Fred Everiss at a very early age, when he scored five goals in his first game for the Albion reserve side. The reward for that performance was immediate promotion to the first team, at Oldham in October 1921, meaning that, at the age of 16 years and 63 days, Wilson became the youngest ever player in a League game for the club – a record which still stands to this day. Wilson took until 1924 to become a regular in the side – when he was the regular inside-left in the Albion team that finished as runners-up to Hubert Chapman's Huddersfield in 1924-25 – although he managed to win three Central League Championship medals with the reserves. By the time Albion were dicing with relegation in 1928, Wilson had gone to Sheffield Wednesday, and he also later played for Aston Villa and Coventry City.

WINS, BEST. Albion's best win in the Football League is a record score that they hold jointly with Nottingham Forest, set on 4 April 1892, when they beat Darwen 12-0 at Stoney Lane. Tom Pearson scored four goals, and Billy Bassett three, as Albion beat the previous League record, of 12-2, set by Aston Villa three weeks before. In the FA Cup, Albion's best win was in an away game, when they won 10-1 at Chatham in the quarter-finals of 1889. In the League Cup, Albion have twice won 6-1, at home to Coventry City in 1965 and at home to Aston Villa the following year. The record victory by an Albion First XI side in any competition came in the Birmingham Senior Cup, first round tie, at home to Coseley in November 1882: 26-0. Albion were 17-0 ahead at half-time, and every outfield player managed to get on the scoresheet.

WINS, SUCCESSIVE. Albion's best run of victories in the League came in 1901-02 when they won ten matches in a row in December and January. After a 1-1 draw at Gainsborough, the side then won another five games in succession on their way to the Second Division Championship.

WOOD, STANLEY. Wood was Albion's outside-left in the 1931 promotion and FA Cup double side. Signed from Winsford United, the speedy winger played nearly 300 games for the club, scoring a useful 66 goals, leaving for Halifax Town when Albion were relegated from the First Division in May 1938.

WOODHALL, GEORGE. West Bromwich-born 'Spry' Woodhall joined the Albion in May 1883, and starred in three consecutive FA Cup finals, 1886, 1887 and 1888, scoring the winning goal in the last game, against Preston North End. Capped twice for England, Woodhall was a clever inside-right or winger who formed a good partnership with Billy Bassett, although their early playing relationship was soured somewhat by Woodhall's remarkable 'boycott' of the younger man – he simply refused to pass to the player who was usurping his position as the Albion's star player! In his nine years at the club, before leaving for a brief spell with neighbours Wolves, Woodhall played in over 200 games, scoring around 90 goals.

WORLD CHAMPIONSHIP. Long before the European Cup was first thought of, much less the 'Inter-Continental Cup' now played for in Tokyo between the Champions of Europe and South America, Albion played in the inaugural 'World Championship' match – in 1888. The game billed as such was a challenge match between the two Cup-winning clubs of the two major football-playing countries at that time – England and Scotland, represented by West Bromwich Albion and Renton, who had beaten Cambuslang 6-1 in the Scottish Cup final. The match, played on 19 May, at Hampden Park, should never have been played, so bad were the weather conditions. So bad, indeed, that, at one point, the referee had to take the players off the field for ten minutes until the heavy thunder and lightning had abated somewhat, and the half-time break was curtailed, in order to get the game over as soon as possible. Indeed, as the neutral Irish referee admitted later, he was thinking of abandoning the game as late as the 80th minute. In the end, Renton won 4-1 thanks to three goals in the space of 15 minutes in the second half, when the downpour was at its worst. Renton were the top side in Scotland at that time, and went on to become founder members of the Scottish Football League, only to be expelled – and disbanded – within a few years as a penalty for playing a match against a professional side. Curiously, Albion were invited to Scotland in 1988 to play in a game to celebrate the centenary of that World Championship challenge match, when they played Second Division Dumbarton, the nearest club side to Renton; Albion lost 2-1.

WORST START. Albion's worst start to a season, as with so many of the more catastrophic club records, came in 1985-86. After drawing their opening Division One game, at home to newcomers Oxford United, they went on to lose the next nine League games, a record number of consecutive defeats which, incidentally, was to stand for only ten years. The losing sequence was broken after the resignation of manager Johnny Giles, Albion gaining a point at home to Tottenham in Nobby Stiles' first game in charge. They did not gain their first League win of the season until their 13th game, on 19 October, when they beat Birmingham City 2-1 at The Hawthorns. The club went on to gain just three more League victories all season, and finished bottom of the First Division.

WYLIE, RON. After Ronnie Allen had been appointed Albion's 'general manager' in 1982, the board made a surprise selection by naming former Coventry City coach (and ex-Villa and Blues defender) Ron Wylie, then player-coach of Hong Kong side, Bulova, as their next manager. Largely unknown outside the Midlands, Wylie, who had impressed as a youth team coach with the Sky Blues, got off to a fair start in the 1982-83 season, when successive wins over Stoke, Manchester United and Brighton saw his side challenging early on, but a final position of 11th was a poor one considering the talent still available at the club. Disputes between the senior players, and Mike Kelly, Wylie's choice of 'hard man' coach, led to discipline problems in the club, which came to a head with a stunning 5-0 home defeat by Nottingham Forest in February 1984, and Wylie and Kelly resigned the fol-

lowing day, to be replaced by Johnny Giles. Wylie returned to
Aston Villa as their reserve team coach, and is now their Officer
for Football in the Community.

XI, ALL-TIME BEST. Albion have had some marvellous players in nearly 120 years of their existence. The following side, playing 4-2-4, with five substitutes, could probably have beaten any side in the world, had it been possible to get all of the players together at their peak: Joe Reader, Don Howe, Jesse Pennington, Charlie Perry, Ray Barlow, Bryan Robson, Johnny Giles, Billy Bassett, Tony Brown, Cyrille Regis, Laurie Cunningham. Subs: Bob Roberts, Derek Statham, John Wile, Ronnie Allen, Jeff Astle.

X-RATED MATCHES. Only one Albion match has ever been abandoned because of trouble on or off the field – the vicious Anglo-Italian Tournament match at Lanerossi Vicenza, in May 1970. Albion midfielder Asa Hartford sparked off a fight on the pitch which ignited a riot on the terraces, and the game was abandoned in the 78th minute, with neither side awarded any points. A fairly close second, though, in the list of Albion X-rated games was the infamous match at Elland Road in April 1971, when the match was stopped after a pitch invasion caused by a dubious Jeff Astle goal which put Albion 2-0 ahead against a Leeds side looking for the championship. Albion had not won an away match for nearly two years. Albion went on to win 2-1, and Arsenal overtook Leeds to win the First Division Championship. As a result of the 'riot', Leeds were forced to play their first three home games of the following season away from home. Not surprisingly, there was a certain amount of 'bad blood' between the two clubs after that infamous game, which spilled over at The Hawthorns in May 1982. Albion beat Leeds 2-0 effectively to relegate the Yorkshire club, and make themselves safe, a result which sparked another serious disturbance in which Leeds fans caused thousands of pounds of damage inside and outside the ground. Five years later, Leeds were again the visitors in another troublesome game which saw three players sent off (including Albion's Carlton Palmer) and ended with the visiting supporters setting fire to wooden buildings in the Smethwick End of the ground.

XMAS DAY. With the small number of holidays available in Victorian times, football clubs had to take every opportunity to maximise revenue, and Christmas Day matches were a regular feature in the early days of professional football, with Albion playing their first Yuletide League game on 25 December 1896 – and Albion lost 8-1 to Derby County! After that result, Albion directors wisely decided not to play on Christmas Day itself for another eight seasons, relenting in 1905, when they drew 1-1 at home to Clapton Orient. The following year, they recorded their first Christmas Day win, 6-1 at home to Grimsby, and it is noticeable that whilst the club arranged Chrismas Day fixtures for the next five years, they made sure they were all at The Hawthorns; and when they next lost such a game, to the Wolves in 1909, they gave the fixture a rest again for another couple of years. Albion played another 21 Christmas Day fixtures until the practice ceased. On 25 December 1956 Newcastle United were the visitors to The Hawthorns, and Albion won 1-0 with a Ray Barlow goal. The folly of Christmas football was fully demonstrated that year, in particular, as both teams then had to hot-foot it back to the north-east for the return game on Boxing Day, less than 24 hours later!

Y

YOUNGEST PLAYER. The youngest player ever to play for the Albion in a League game is Charles Wilson, who made his Albion first team debut at Oldham in October 1921. He was 73 days past his 16th birthday. As a 15-year-old, Wilson had scored five goals in a 6-0 win in his first game for the Albion reserve side. Wilson, however, is not the youngest player to appear for the club in any competitive game. That distinction belongs to Frank Hodgetts, who was 16 years and 26 days when he played for the Albion at home to Notts County in a Wartime League South game in October 1940.

YOUTH. As one of the less wealthy clubs in the country, Albion have long had to rely on an efficient youth policy to try to recruit new talent cheaply. Many of the club's greatest players – Billy Bassett, Jesse Pennington, Bryan Robson, Derek Statham, Bobby Hope, Alistair Robertson, Graham Williams, Tony Brown – were home-grown talent, coming up through the club's youth sides. Albion have also done very well in the FA Youth Cup, a competition for under-18 sides launched in 1952. In 1954, Albion reached the Youth Cup semi-final, losing 7-1 on aggregate to Manchester United. The following year the side went one better, but again lost to Manchester United, in the final, again by a 7-1 aggregate score. In 1969, Albion won the first leg of the final 3-0 against

Sunderland at The Hawthorns, but lost the second leg 6-0, after having two men sent off. In 1976, Albion won the FA Youth Cup for the first time, beating Wolves 5-0 on aggregate. It is no coincidence that Albion's youth policy has deteriorated badly in the last ten years – since trainer Albert McPherson was released by Johnny Giles in favour of Nobby Stiles – in parallel with the club's general decline on the field. Where there was once a veritable production line of top quality young players, such as Asa Hartford, Len Cantello, Dave Burrows and Carlton Palmer, now there is nothing, with only Daryl Burgess in the current side a product of the Albion 'nursery'.

YUGOSLAVIA. Albion's first foray into Yugoslavia was during a pre-season tour of the country in 1971, when they played Hadjuk Split (1-2), FK Velez (3-2) and FK Sarajevo (1-1). Bobby Gould scored in each game. In 1978-79, Albion were drawn away to crack Yugoslav side Red Star Belgrade in the first leg of their UEFA quarter-final tie, and lost 1-0 to a free-kick goal late in the game. Albion took an early lead in the home game, but fell to a sucker punch in the last two minutes, and lost 2-1 on aggregate. In February 1981, Albion invited Red Star back to The Hawthorns for a friendly on their British tour, and Albion won 4-2. In August 1980, Albion competed in the round-robin Marjan Trophy in Split. In their first game they lost 5-1 to the host side, Hadjuk Split, and followed that up with a goalless draw against Swiss side FC Zurich. Albion have had two Yugoslavian internationals on trial. In 1979, goalkeeper Ivan Katalinic played in goal for the Albion in their centenary game against Ajax, at The Hawthorns, whilst a year later, Yugoslavian midfielder Drazen Muzinic played – and scored – in a pre-season win at Swindon. Neither player was signed.

Z

ZENITH DS CUP. Albion only played two matches, both at home, in the awkwardly named Zenith Data Systems Cup, which was the new name for the ill-fated Simod Cup. In 1989, First Division Derby County, inspired by a Dean Saunders hat-trick, won 5-0, and a year later, Barnsley, with a hat-trick from former Albion midfielder Ian Banks, won 5-3. Albion's relegation five months later meant that they could no longer compete in the competition, which was reserved for First and Second Division sides only.

ZONDERVAN, ROMEO. The poetically named Zondervan was signed by Ronnie Allen from Twente Enschede near the end of the 1981-82 season, in a bid to shore up a talented side that was fast slipping towards the Second Division. Although a skilful, mobile midfielder, Zondervan made his Albion debut at Middlesbrough in March 1982 as a left-back. He never really got to grips with the relegation battle, and was left out of the side for the vital last four matches, two of which were won to ensure Albion's survival. The Dutchman's form improved under new manager Ron Wylie, although it took him 32 games to score his first goal – but he rarely looked convincing, even in partnership with Albion's other Dutch import, Maarten Jol, although he managed to clock up nearly 100 appearances for the club. Once Johnny Giles took over in February 1984, both Jol and Zondervan lasted just three games before they were permanently discarded, Zondervan signing for Ipswich the following month for £70,000 – a £150,000 loss for Albion. Once at Portman Road, though, Zondervan seemed to bloom, and he was guaranteed to excel against the Albion, in particular, controlling the midfield in a way which would have seemed impossible at The Hawthorns. He later moved back to Holland to end his career in 1992, after playing more than 300 games for the Suffolk side.